Collins

Enhanced English Alive Coursebook 4

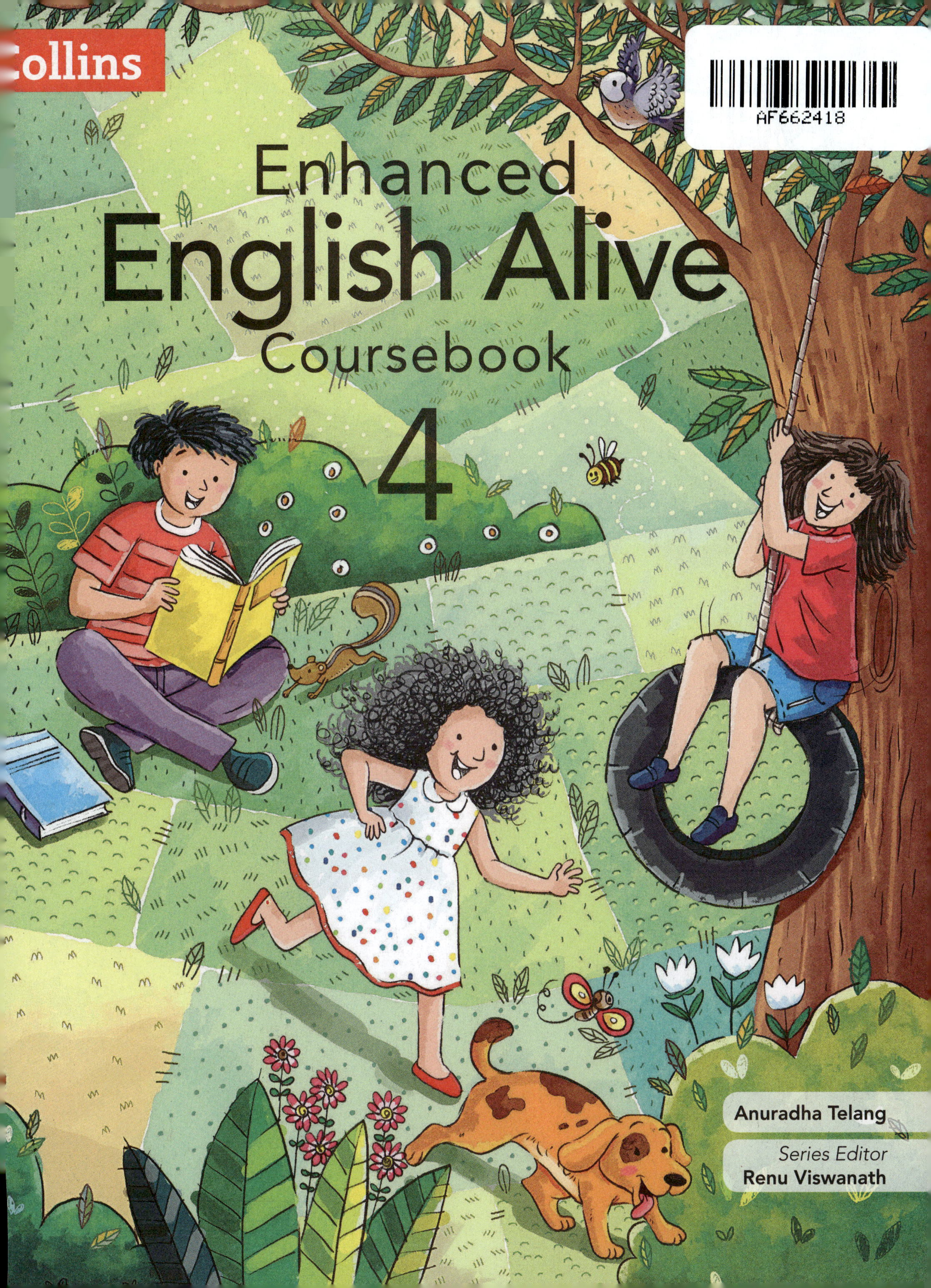

Anuradha Telang

Series Editor
Renu Viswanath

Acknowledgements

The publishers wish to thank and acknowledge the following for granting us permission to use copyright material:

The Will (English), translated by Pragya Gopinath, based on original story *Vaseeyat* (Urdu), written by Aniz Azmi, supported by P.A.N.I Foundation, published by Pratham Books (© Pratham Books, 2015) under a CC BY 4.0 license on StoryWeaver.

The publishers have applied for permission for the following:
I'm Late for School by Gareth Lancaster; *Shadow and Carly* by Janet Slike; *The Potter* by Chitra Padmanabhan; *Liza and the Lost Letter* by Bruce Lansky
Acknowledgements for these texts will be made in the future editions of the book.

Every effort has been made to trace copyright holders and to obtain their permission for the use of copyright material. However, in some instances, we have been unable to trace the owners of the copyright pieces published here. The authors and publishers will gladly receive any information enabling them to rectify any error or omission in subsequent editions.

Illustrations

Cover and Title Page: Created by Toonfantasy

Inside: Page 17: FARBAI; **28:** SpicyTruffel; **29:** norwayblue; **46:** pcturner71; **47:** Daria Ustiugova; **48:** winhorse, miya227, jiratto, mura, zeremski, sergio_kumer; **58:** Nataleana; **59:** VectorStory; **63:** Vasilchuck; **77:** ePhotocorp; **78:** VisualCommunications; **84:** pickbiz; **102:** Looper_cro, colematt, Svetlana Aganina; **106:** Web Gallery of Art/Public domain, gallery.euroweb.hu/Public domain.

Preface

Enhanced English Alive is a multi-skill course in English that adheres to the guidelines laid down by the **National Education Policy, 2020**. This edition retains the original essence of teaching communicative English using a cross-curricular approach and interactive and experiential teaching and learning methods. It offers high-quality English language materials with a coherent structured approach, effective integration of subject knowledge and life skills.

The series comprises Coursebooks and Workbooks for Foundational Stage (Nursery, LKG, UKG, Classes 1 and 2), Preparatory Stage (Classes 3 to 5), and Middle Stage (Classes 6 to 8). Literature Readers are for the Preparatory and Middle Stages (Classes 3 to 8). Each grade package includes a Teacher's Resource Pack and a Collins DigiSuite.

This series integrates the essence of **NIPUN Bharat** guidelines, which extensively deal with foundational literacy and numeracy. Each book aims to motivate learners to read independently, to improve their vocabulary, to develop their critical thinking and creative skills, as well as to enhance their ability to express themselves both verbally and in writing.

This series takes care of the requirements of **Structured Assessments For Analyzing Learning (SAFAL)**. Research-based activities and projects have been used to instill inquiry-based learning, while comprehension passages have been followed by extrapolative and value-based questions that involve analysis-based learning. Additionally, in the Middle Stage (Classes 6 to 8), an end-of year question paper is provided which is based on the latest CBSE guidelines.

Key features

Coursebooks

- **Warm-up:** A wide variety of picture-based fun activities or probing questions at the beginning of chapters initiate the learner into the subject and ensure his/her active engagement in the lesson. For grades 1 to 5, these activities are introspective and meditative inquiries that are based on the pedagogy of mindfulness as delineated in the NEP, 2020.
- **Reading:** Each book has well-chosen selections from a wide range of literary genres that are also useful in cross-curricular teaching. These include picture stories and comic strips.
- **Cross-curricular boxes:** This series specially covers topics that are interrelated with other subjects taught in the same grade. Dedicated boxes teaching these cross-curricular concepts are placed along the main text.
- **Glossary:** All new words in the text are highlighted and their meanings are given in simple language using the easiest possible words. Literary devices are also taught along with a glossary of literary terms.
- **Summary:** A short summary at the end of each text is provided for an easy way to remember the essence of the text.
- **Comprehension:** This section includes plenty of exercises including factual, inferential, **and** extrapolative questions.
- **Life Skills and Values:** There is a separate thematic section on life skills and values aimed at developing good character in students and equipping them with skills needed to cope with

different challenges in life. Guidelines set by NEP, 2020 have been followed in selecting these life skills and values.

- **Vocabulary:** Each chapter has boxed explanations of new vocabulary words and topics followed by a variety of exercises. Spelling is also taught in this section with proper rules and explanations. Moreover, dictionary skills are taught in books 3 to 8.
- **Grammar:** Grade-appropriate grammar is explained with several visual models and extensive examples from the learner's immediate world. Plenty of varied exercises follow them to ensure the learner has learnt the concept well.
- **Listening and Speaking:** This section aims at developing students' listening, speaking, and overall communicative skills through a wide variety of tasks and pair/group activities. Pronunciation is also covered in this section in books 3 to 8.
- **Writing:** This well-graded section has a variety of age-appropriate creative and scaffolded writing tasks. These cover informal and formal letters, diary entries, flow charts, posters, stories, biographies, notices, reports, travelogues, character sketches, book reviews, recipes, acrostic poems, articles, and picture-based compositions.
- **Activities:** There is a fun activity accompanying each poem. Most of these activities require working collaboratively in groups or pairs. These activities are varied and cover various twenty-first century life skills.
- **Projects:** Three well-designed cross-curricular projects are provided that are linked to topics taught in that particular grade in other subjects.
- **Cross-curricular Vocabulary:** A word bank teaching cross-curricular vocabulary is included at the end of books 3 to 5. Words are classified according to different subjects and categories.

Workbooks

The Workbooks have been carefully mapped to the Coursebooks, and created with the intention of independent learning. Each Workbook has 8 comprehension passages including poems. The vocabulary and grammar sections include a quick recap of the concepts covered in the corresponding chapter of the Coursebook. The listening, speaking, and writing sections allow learners extra practice. Additional assessment papers included in the Workbooks are patterned on the Structured Assessments For Analyzing Learning (SAFAL). These offer a scope for assessing the competencies of critical thinking, inquiry-based learning, and analysis-based learning.

Literature Readers

The Literature Readers teach critical appreciation of literature through short stories, folktales, fairytales, poems and extracts from classics from the literature of different ages. A summary at the end offers a revision and understanding of the essence of the text. Literary devices are also taught along with a glossary of literary terms.

Teacher's Resource Pack

The Teacher's Resource Pack contain model lesson plans, additional worksheets, and grammar-based projects covering all the pedagogical aspects included in the Coursebooks, along with listening texts and answer keys to all exercises across Coursebooks, Workbooks, Literature Readers, and additional assessment papers.

Key to Icons

Enhanced English Alive is a multi-skill course that is closely aligned with the National Education Policy, 2020. It uses an interactive approach, cross-curricular themes, and experiential activities to build communicative competence in students. This series aims to prepare learners with the various skills outlined in the National Education Policy, 2020. These skills have been tagged appropriately with easily recognizable icons for the user's convenience. Here is the key to all the icons used in this series.

Cross-Curricular Content

- The cross-curricular approach to a topic recognizes that all subjects are interlinked. It includes contributions from several different disciplines or viewpoints for effective learning.
- All chapters have dedicated boxes teaching cross-curricular content appropriate to that class. These boxes cover the following:

Science Scan covers topics related to science.

Maths Magic covers topics related to mathematics.

Earth Speak covers topics related to geography and environmental studies.

Looking Back covers topics related to historical events and personalities.

Fact File covers topics related to general knowledge and awareness.

Lit Bits covers topics related to literature and famous literary figures.

Art and Culture covers topics related to art and culture.

Twenty-First Century Skills

- The twenty-first century skills ensure that today's students can thrive in an ever-changing world and can use these skills to learn constantly.
- Here are the most commonly cited twenty-first century skills in this series:

21st Century Skills — Critical Thinking: Critical Thinking

21st Century Skills — Communication: Communication Skills

21st Century Skills — Collaboration: Collaboration

21st Century Skills — Creative Thinking: Creativity

21st Century Skills — ICT: Information Communication Technology Skills or Digital Literacy

Experiential Learning

- Experiential learning is a process of learning through hands-on experience. Here, students 'learn by doing' an activity followed by reflective observation on the experience from multiple perspectives.
- This method helps learners link existing knowledge to understand new concepts and apply it to make decisions.

Art Integration

- Art Integrated Learning (AIL) is a teaching-learning model that integrates fine arts (painting, sculpture, architecture, music, and poetry), performing arts (theatre and dance), and photography with teaching new concepts.
- This provides students with an experiential and a multi-disciplinary learning experience.

Happiness Content

- Learning should be an enjoyable process for learners. It should focus on building and understanding new concepts rather than rote learning.
- Children should experience happiness through learning and awareness, active participation in class, and also in their relationships with their friends and family.

India Focus

- India Focus puts spotlight on the heritage, culture, customs, and history and geography of the Indian subcontinent.
- This provides students a deeper understanding of their homeland and creates a sense of solidarity.

Sustainable Development Goals

- The Sustainable Development Goals, adopted by the United Nations in 2015, are a collection of 17 interlinked global goals designed to achieve a better and more sustainable future for all by 2030. Here are the 17 goals:

Key Features

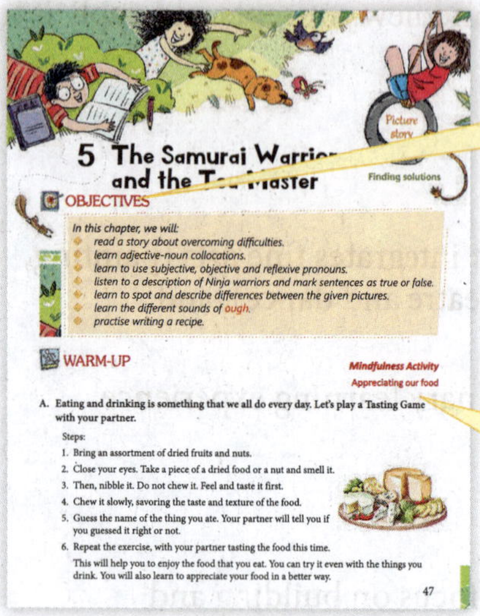
5 The Samurai Warrior and the Tea Master

OBJECTIVES

In this chapter, we will:
- read a story about overcoming difficulties.
- learn adjective-noun collocations.
- learn to use subjective, objective and reflexive pronouns.
- listen to a description of Ninja warriors and mark sentences as true or false.
- learn to spot and describe differences between the given pictures.
- learn the different sounds of ough.
- practise writing a recipe.

WARM-UP

Mindfulness Activity
Appreciating our food

A. Eating and drinking is something that we all do every day. Let's play a Tasting Game with your partner.

Steps:
1. Bring an assortment of dried fruits and nuts.
2. Close your eyes. Take a piece of a dried food or a nut and smell it.
3. Then, nibble it. Do not chew it. Feel and taste it first.
4. Chew it slowly, savoring the taste and texture of the food.
5. Guess the name of the thing you ate. Your partner will tell you if you guessed it right or not.
6. Repeat the exercise, with your partner tasting the food this time.

This will help you to enjoy the food that you eat. You can try it even with the things you drink. You will also learn to appreciate your food in a better way.

47

Page 47

Objectives: All learning goals for the chapter listed out

Comprehension: Covers factual, inferential, and extrapolative questions

Warm-up: Mindfulness activities to help train the student's mind to be involved in the present moment without getting distracted, followed by theme-based warm-ups

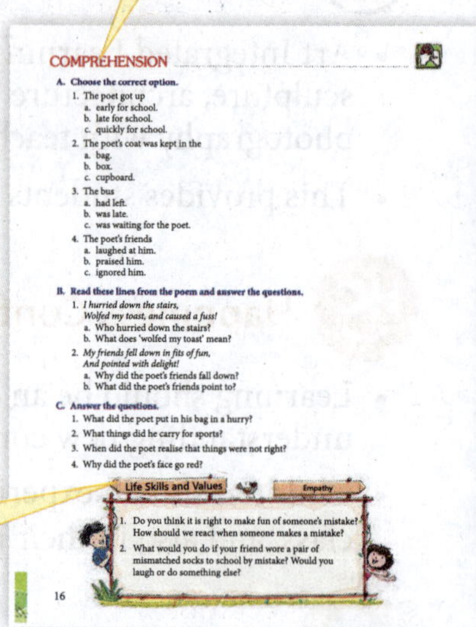
COMPREHENSION

A. Choose the correct option.
1. The poet got up
a. early for school.
b. late for school.
c. quickly for school.
2. The poet's coat was kept in the
a. bag.
b. box.
c. cupboard.
3. The bus
a. had left.
b. was late.
c. was waiting for the poet.
4. The poet's friends
a. laughed at him.
b. praised him.
c. ignored him.

B. Read these lines from the poem and answer the questions.
1. *I hurried down the stairs, Wolfed my toast, and caused a fuss!*
a. Who hurried down the stairs?
b. What does 'wolfed my toast' mean?
2. *My friends fell down in fits of fun, And pointed with delight!*
a. Why did the poet's friends fall down?
b. What did the poet's friends point to?

C. Answer the questions.
1. What did the poet put in his bag in a hurry?
2. What things did he carry for sports?
3. When did the poet realise that things were not right?
4. Why did the poet's face go red?

Life Skills and Values — Empathy
1. Do you think it is right to make fun of someone's mistake? How should we react when someone makes a mistake?
2. What would you do if your friend wore a pair of mismatched socks to school by mistake? Would you laugh or do something else?

16

Life Skills and Values: Value-based questions to develop good character through experiential learning

Page 16

Reading: A good balance of Indian and global selections from a wide range of literary genres that are useful in cross-curricular teaching

Cross-curricular boxes: Topics related to other subjects highlighted

Glossary: Meanings for new words and literary devices given alongside the text

READING

Read this story about Anjali and her friend Pinky. The two friends prove that everything is possible if you set your mind to it.

Anjali's parents had moved to Junagarh a month ago. Her father, Ashish, was the commissioner of the city. Her mother, Suman, worked with a bank. Anjali had simply fallen in love with the lush green city. She especially enjoyed the lion safari at the Sasan-Gir Sanctuary, which was just two hours' drive away.

Anjali was eager to join her new school. It was Friday and the school was to reopen on Monday after the vacation. She went to the living room and flopped herself on the settee, her favourite haunt to read storybooks.

Late in the afternoon, she heard someone enter her house. Her mother informed her that it was Raghuram. He was the gardener who lived in the outhouse located in the mango orchard behind their home. He had brought some fresh mangoes.

Anjali loved mangoes and she jumped up with joy. 'Hurrah!' She grabbed a mango in each hand and ran off to the garden swing to enjoy the juicy fruit. As she was swinging, she saw a timid face peep from behind the tree.

She called out, 'Who are you?'

Fact File
- Sasan-Gir or Gir National Park is a wildlife sanctuary. It is the only place in Asia where Asiatic lions are found.
- Lions are found on only two continents – Africa and Asia.
- Asiatic lions are a highly endangered species, and less than 400 of them are left in Sasan-Gir.

commissioner: the head of a city administration
lush green: if you describe a place as lush green, it means that place has a lot of trees and plants
safari: a trip to see wild animals
flopped: sat down heavily and suddenly
settee: a long seat with a back and arms
haunt: a place frequently visited by a person
outhouse: a building such as a shed that is built on or in the grounds of a house
timid: (here) shy and nervous

19

Page 19

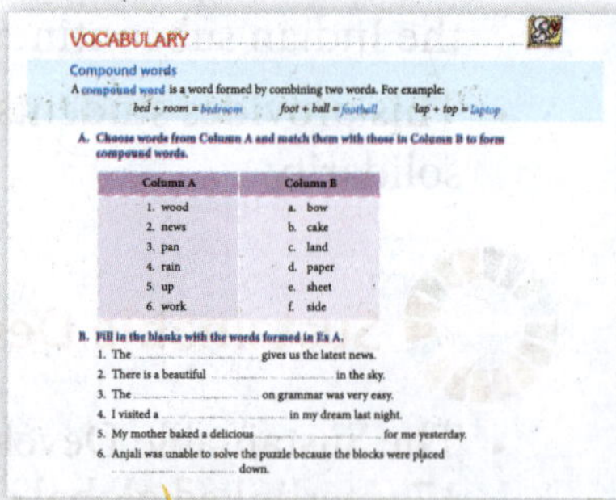
VOCABULARY

Compound words

A compound word is a word formed by combining two words. For example:
bed + room = bedroom   foot + ball = football   lap + top = laptop

A. Choose words from Column A and match them with those in Column B to form compound words.

Column A	Column B
1. wood	a. bow
2. news	b. cake
3. pan	c. land
4. rain	d. paper
5. up	e. sheet
6. work	f. side

B. Fill in the blanks with the words formed in Ex A.
1. The .... gives us the latest news.
2. There is a beautiful .... in the sky.
3. The .... on grammar was very easy.
4. I visited a .... in my dream last night.
5. My mother baked a delicious .... for me yesterday.
6. Anjali was unable to solve the puzzle because the blocks were placed .... down.

Page 23

Vocabulary: Covers language skills with focus on usage

Summary: A short summary at the end of each text for a mental revision and an easier way of remembering the essence of the text

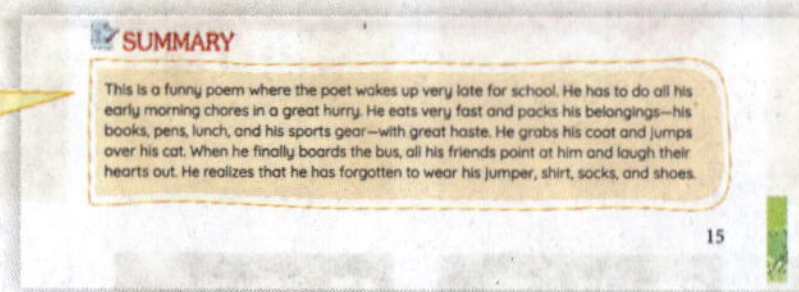
SUMMARY

This is a funny poem where the poet wakes up very late for school. He has to do all his early morning chores in a great hurry. He eats very fast and packs his belongings—his books, pens, lunch, and his sports gear—with great haste. He grabs his coat and jumps over his cat. When he finally boards the bus, all his friends point at him and laugh their hearts out. He realizes that he has forgotten to wear his jumper, shirt, socks, and shoes.

15

Page 15

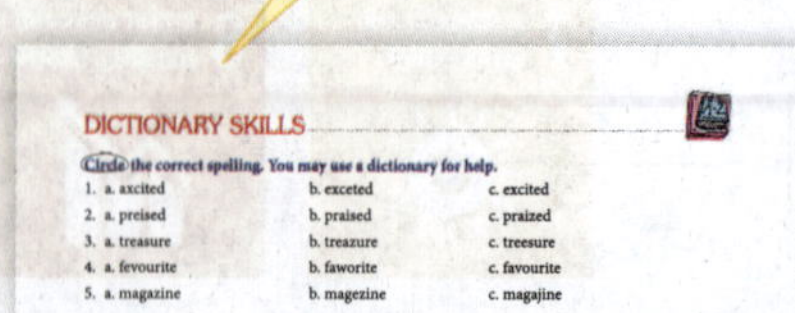
DICTIONARY SKILLS

Circle the correct spelling. You may use a dictionary for help.

1. a. excited	b. exceted	c. exited
2. a. preised	b. praised	c. praized
3. a. treasure	b. treasure	c. treesure
4. a. frvourite	b. favorite	c. favourite
5. a. magazine	b. magezine	c. magajine

Page 24

Grammar: Grade-appropriate grammar explained with several visual models and extensive examples, followed by exercises

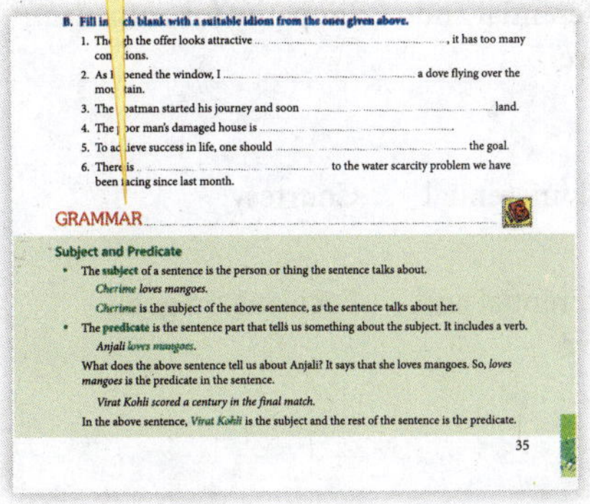
B. Fill in each blank with a suitable idiom from the ones given above.

1. Though the offer looks attractive ...., it has too many conditions.
2. As I opened the window, I .... a dove flying over the mountain.
3. The batman started his journey and soon .... land.
4. The poor man's damaged house is ....
5. To achieve success in life, one should .... the goal.
6. There is .... to the water scarcity problem we have been facing since last month.

GRAMMAR

Subject and Predicate

- The **subject** of a sentence is the person or thing the sentence talks about.
  Cherime loves mangoes.
  Cherime is the subject of the above sentence, as the sentence talks about her.
- The **predicate** is the sentence part that tells us something about the subject. It includes a verb.
  Anjali loves mangoes.

What does the above sentence tell us about Anjali? It says that she loves mangoes. So, *loves mangoes* is the predicate in the sentence.

Virat Kohli scored a century in the final match.

In the above sentence, *Virat Kohli* is the subject and the rest of the sentence is the predicate.

35

Page 35

Writing: A well-graded section with a variety of creative and scaffolded writing tasks:

- letter writing
- diary entry
- flow charts
- poster making
- biography
- notice writing
- report-writing
- travelogue writing
- character sketch
- book review
- recipe writing
- acrostic poem
- description writing
- picture composition

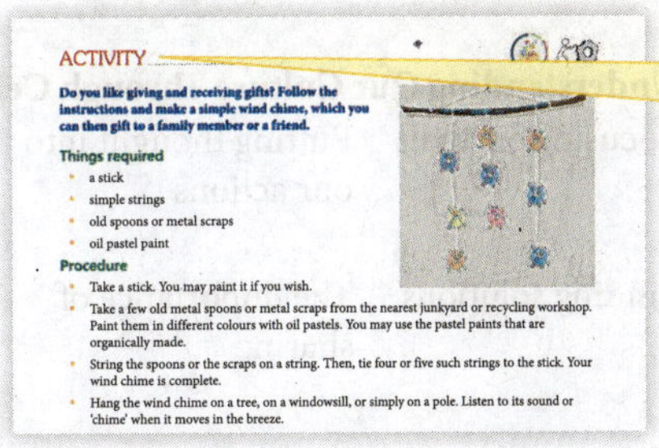
ACTIVITY

Do you like giving and receiving gifts? Follow the instructions and make a simple wind chime, which you can then gift to a family member or a friend.

Things required

- a stick
- simple strings
- old spoons or metal scraps
- oil pastel paint

Procedure

- Take a stick. You may paint it if you wish.
- Take a few old metal spoons or metal scraps from the nearest junkyard or recycling workshop. Paint them in different colours with oil pastels. You may use the pastel paints that are organically made.
- String the spoons or the scraps on a string. Then, tie four or five such strings to the stick. Your wind chime is complete.
- Hang the wind chime on a tree, on a windowsill, or simply on a pole. Listen to its sound or 'chime' when it moves in the breeze.

Page 46

Activity: A collaborative fun activity with each poem

Listening and Speaking: A wide variety of communicative activities leading to collaboration and team building; also covers pronunciation

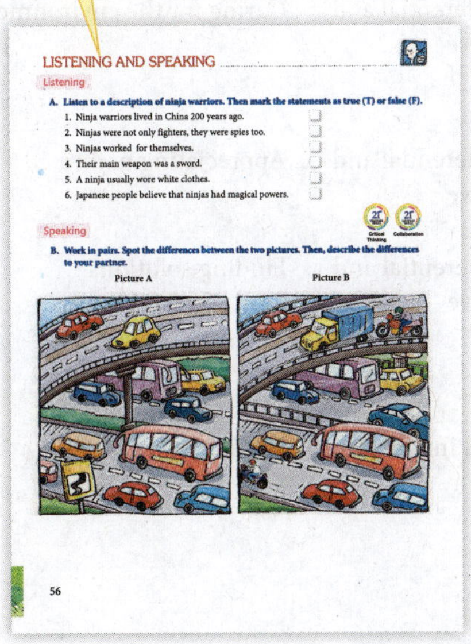
LISTENING AND SPEAKING

Listening

A. Listen to a description of ninja warriors. Then mark the statements as true (T) or false (F).

1. Ninja warriors lived in China 200 years ago.
2. Ninjas were not only fighters, they were spies too.
3. Ninjas worked for themselves.
4. Their main weapon was a sword.
5. A ninja usually wore white clothes.
6. Japanese people believe that ninjas had magical powers.

Speaking

B. Work in pairs. Spot the differences between the two pictures. Then, describe the differences to your partner.

Picture A Picture B

56

Page 56

Project: Three cross-curricular projects linked to topics taught in other subjects in this grade

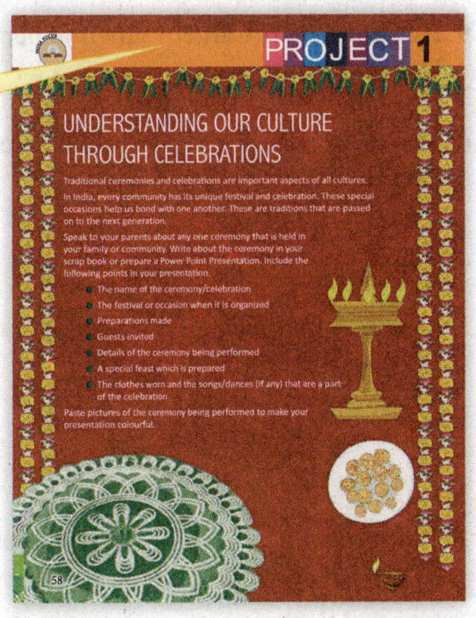
PROJECT 1

UNDERSTANDING OUR CULTURE THROUGH CELEBRATIONS

Traditional ceremonies and celebrations are important aspects of all cultures.

In India, every community has its unique festival and celebration. These special occasions help us bond with one another. These are traditions that are passed on to the next generation.

Speak to your parents about any one ceremony that is held in your family or community. Write about the ceremony in your scrap book or prepare a Power Point Presentation. Include the following points in your presentation.

- The name of the ceremony/celebration
- The festival or occasion when it is organized
- Preparations made
- Guests invited
- Details of the ceremony being performed
- A special feast which is prepared
- The clothes worn and the songs/dances (if any) that are a part of the celebration

Paste pictures of the ceremony being performed to make your presentation colourful.

58

Page 58

*This series integrates the essence of **NIPUN Bharat** guidelines and the requirements of **Structured Assessments For Analyzing Learning (SAFAL)**.*

Detailed Contents

Vocabulary	Grammar	Listening and Speaking	Writing /Activity
• Rhyming words			• Answering questions on time
• Compound words • Choosing the correct spelling	• Articles (indefinite and definite) • Prepositions of time (*in*, *on*, *at*)	• Listening to a poem and gap-filling • Telling a chain story	• Imaginative writing
• Friendship terms • Idioms	• Subject and predicate • *Punctuation:* comma, full stop, question mark, exclamation mark	• Listening and gap-filling • Making and responding to requests	• Writing an informal letter
• Cardinal and ordinal numbers			• Making a wind chime
• Collocations: adjectives and nouns	• Personal pronouns: subjective, objective and reflexive	• Listening to a description and marking true or false • Describing differences between two pictures • Eight different pronunciations of *ough*	• Writing the recipe of lemon ice tea
• Literary device: Rhyme scheme			• Expressing your goals through pictures with a caption for each stage
• Prefixes • Making antonyms using prefixes • Searching for word meanings in a dictionary	• Words used as nouns and verbs • Comparative adjectives	• Listening to announcements at a railway station and filling in a table • Making suggestions	• Writing a character sketch
• Suffixes • Forming adjectives by adding suffixes to the root word	• *Will* and *can* • *Some* and *any*	• Listening to an announcement and filling in a form • Describing a family vacation picture	• Writing a report on a cleanliness drive in your neighbourhood
• Synonyms and antonyms			• Making a leaf family
• Proverbs	• *Should* and *shouldn't* • Making offers using *Let me* / *Let us* + verbs	• Listening for details and filling up a form • Providing suggestions for a birthday party using *Let me* and *Let us*	• Writing a travelogue
• Portmanteau words • Spellings: doubling the final letter l	• Subject-verb agreement • Simple past and past continuous tenses	• Listening and sequencing events from the life of Rani Lakshmibai • Requesting to help a poor child • Pronouncing the short *o* sound	• Writing a biography of a family member
• Simile • Antonyms			• Group work on materials that are used to make pots
• British and American English • Gender	• Types of sentences: declarative, imperative, exclamatory and interrogative	• Listening and summarising in short sentences • Giving directions	• Writing a review of the play

Contents

1 I'm Late for School

Self and friends

OBJECTIVES

In this chapter, we will:

- *read and understand a humorous poem.*
- *understand the importance of sympathy.*
- *learn rhyming words.*
- *learn to keep time.*

WARM-UP

Mindfulness Activity
Being mindful of time and routine

A. Work in pairs. Look at the picture of Rohan's room. Discuss it with your partner.

B. Look at your own bag. Answer these questions.

1. Have you packed your things neatly?
2. Have you put your books and other belongings properly?
3. Did you pack your bag well in time or hurriedly in the morning?

Close your eyes and think about your answers. Write down in your notebook how you will prepare yourself for school the next day.

READING

Read this funny poem by Gareth Lancaster about a boy who wakes up late one day. Find out what happens.

I got up late for school today,
And nearly missed the bus!
I hurried down the stairs,
Wolfed my toast, and caused a fuss!

wolfed: (here) ate quickly, in a hurry
fuss: when many things are done at the same time and in a hurry, causing worry

I quickly threw books in my bag,
My pens, my lunch and shorts.
Grabbed my coat from out the cupboard,
Took my bat and ball for sports.

I slid across the kitchen floor,
And hopped around the cat!
Then expertly rolled over,
Jumped back up and grabbed my hat!

I belted out of our front door,
Spun round and swung it shut.
Saw the bus was waiting for me,
I felt I had time to strut!

I climbed aboard and then froze still,
And knew that things weren't right!
My friends fell down in fits of fun,
And pointed with delight!

My face went red, I couldn't breathe,
For in my haste I knew!
I'd forgotten to wear trousers,
Jumper, shirt, my socks and shoes!

belted: moved somewhere very quickly
strut: to walk in a proud way with your head held high and your chest out
fits of fun: (here) a short period of time spent laughing
jumper: a warm, knitted piece of clothing which is worn like a T-shirt

SUMMARY

This is a funny poem where the poet wakes up very late for school. He has to do all his early morning chores in a great hurry. He eats very fast and packs his belongings—his books, pens, lunch, and his sports gear—with great haste. He grabs his coat and jumps over his cat. When he finally boards the bus, all his friends point at him and laugh their hearts out. He realizes that he has forgotten to wear his jumper, shirt, socks, and shoes.

COMPREHENSION

A. Choose the correct option.

1. The poet got up
   a. early for school.
   b. late for school.
   c. quickly for school.
2. The poet's coat was kept in the
   a. bag.
   b. box.
   c. cupboard.
3. The bus
   a. had left.
   b. was late.
   c. was waiting for the poet.
4. The poet's friends
   a. laughed at him.
   b. praised him.
   c. ignored him.

B. Read these lines from the poem and answer the questions.

1. *I hurried down the stairs,*
   Wolfed my toast, and caused a fuss!
   a. Who hurried down the stairs?
   b. What does 'wolfed my toast' mean?
2. *My friends fell down in fits of fun,*
   And pointed with delight!
   a. Why did the poet's friends fall down?
   b. What did the poet's friends point to?

C. Answer the questions.

1. What did the poet put in his bag in a hurry?
2. What things did he carry for sports?
3. When did the poet realise that things were not right?
4. Why did the poet's face go red?

Life Skills and Values — **Empathy**

1. Do you think it is right to make fun of someone's mistake? How should we react when someone makes a mistake?
2. What would you do if your friend wore a pair of mismatched socks to school by mistake? Would you laugh or do something else?

VOCABULARY

Rhyming words

- The words *bus* and *fuss* have similar final/ending sounds. When two words have similar final/ending sounds, we say they **rhyme**.

Find three more pairs of words in the poem that rhyme.

1. ....
2. ....
3. ....

ACTIVITY

Critical Thinking

Here are three clocks. Answer the first part of each question by drawing the hands on the clocks to show the time. For the second part, write the answer in the blanks.

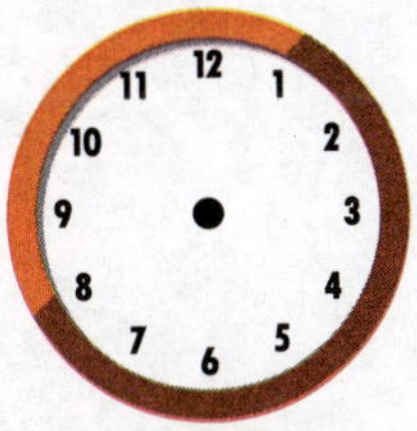

1. When do you wake up? How long do you take to dress up for school?

....

....

....

2. When do you return from school? What do you do after coming home?

....

....

....

3. When do you have dinner? How long does it take you to prepare for bedtime?

....

....

....

4. Before you sleep, do you think about what you did the entire day? Did you waste your time on unimportant things? Could you have spent it in a better way? Write your honest opinion in the space provided below.

....

....

....

....

....

Short story

2 Everything Is Possible

Helping others

OBJECTIVES

In this chapter, we will:

- *read a story about helping others.*
- *learn to use compound words.*
- *learn to spell words correctly.*
- *learn to use articles a, an, and the; and prepositions of time.*
- *listen to a poem and fill in the blanks.*
- *learn to create a chain story.*
- *write a paragraph on helping others.*

WARM-UP

Mindfulness Activity
Importance of caring for others

A. Do you think we can be happy by making others happy? If so, why does it make you happy? Discuss this with your partner.

B. Write two to three things that made you feel happy since morning.

Things that made you feel happy since morning

4 QUALITY EDUCATION

READING

Read this story about Anjali and her friend Pinky. The two friends prove that everything is possible if you set your mind to it.

Anjali's parents had moved to Junagarh a month ago. Her father, Ashish, was the commissioner of the city. Her mother, Suman, worked with a bank. Anjali had simply fallen in love with the lush green city. She especially enjoyed the lion safari at the Sasan-Gir Sanctuary, which was just two hours' drive away from Junagarh.

Anjali was eager to join her new school. It was Friday and the school was to reopen on Monday after the vacation. She went to the living room and flopped herself on the settee, her favourite haunt to read storybooks.

Late in the afternoon, she heard someone enter her house. Her mother informed her that it was Raghuram. He was the gardener who lived in the outhouse located in the mango orchard behind their home. He had brought some fresh mangoes.

Anjali loved mangoes and she jumped up with joy. 'Hurrah!' She grabbed a mango in each hand and ran off to the garden swing to enjoy the juicy fruit. As she was swinging, she saw a timid face peep from behind the tree.

She called out, 'Who are you?'

Fact File

- Sasan-Gir or Gir National Park is a wildlife sanctuary. It is the only place in Asia where Asiatic lions are found.
- Lions are found on only two continents—Africa and Asia.
- Asiatic lions are a highly endangered species, and less than 400 of them are left in Sasan-Gir.

commissioner: the head of a city administration
lush green: if you describe a lace as lush green, it means that place has a lot of trees and plants
safari: a trip to see wild animals
flopped: sat down heavily and suddenly
settee: a long seat with a back and arms
haunt: a place frequently visited by a person
outhouse: a building such as a shed that is built on or in the grounds of a house
timid: (here) shy and nervous

'I am Pinky. My father works in the mango orchard.'

Anjali invited her to play with her on the swing and shared a mango with her.

Many days went by and both the girls became very good friends. One day, Anjali asked, 'I have never seen you go to school. Why?' Pinky looked very uncomfortable. She did not answer and simply ran away.

Anjali was puzzled. The next day, too, there was no sign of Pinky. Anjali missed her friend, and decided to go with her mother and meet Pinky at the outhouse.

As they were walking to Pinky's house, Anjali saw some men put up a new hoarding across the compound wall. It read: **Each one, Teach one.**

Anjali read it and remembered, 'Our teacher has taught us rhyming words. *Teach* and *each* is a pair of rhyming words, but I wonder what this sentence means.'

Suman smiled at her daughter and said, 'It means every person can help another person to read and write.'

'It is a very nice idea!' exclaimed Anjali.

'Yes, indeed it is,' said Suman.

Suman and Anjali reached the outhouse. Pinky met them and shyly said, 'I ran away that day because I thought you would make fun of me. You see, I never went to school and do not know how to read and write. It is impossible that I can learn now.'

'Nothing is impossible, Pinky. In fact, everything is possible if you set your mind to it,' said Suman and put her arms around the child.

Anjali exclaimed, 'I have an idea. Why don't you come home every afternoon after I return from school? I will help you learn how to read and write.'

Fact File

'Each one, teach one' is a proverb which originated in the United States of America during the time African slaves were denied education. When one of these slaves managed to get an education, it was his or her duty to teach another person to read and write.

uncomfortable: worried or nervous

hoarding: a large board at the side of the road or on top of buildings, to show advertisements

Anjali was true to her word and Pinky never missed a day. During the monsoon showers, both the girls stayed indoors and practised reading and writing.

Anjali introduced Pinky to the world of stories. There were many kinds of stories—fairy tales, mythological stories, and Aesop's Fables. Every day, Anjali would bring new books from the school library and read them to Pinky. She even gave Pinky all her old storybooks.

Pinky was unstoppable. She was hard-working and slowly started to read on her own. One day, Suman told Anjali, 'I think now the time has come that Pinky can be admitted to a school.' Anjali was very excited at the idea. 'Do you think she can come to my school?' asked Anjali. Suman enquired and finally Anjali's school was ready to admit her.

Pinky was nervous, but Anjali held her hand firmly and walked her up to her classroom on the first day. There was a slight hint of a tear in Pinky's eyes when Anjali finally waved her goodbye.

That day, Anjali was eagerly waiting near the school gate to know how Pinky had fared on her first day at school. She saw Pinky rushing outside excitedly. She was shouting with joy, 'I did it! I can read, write, and play! I enjoy going to school.'

Just guess who was the happiest person? It was Anjali! She felt as if she had cleared an exam! The two girls sang in chorus, 'Everything is possible!'

mythological: a myth is a well-known story to explain natural events or religious beliefs. Anything related to myths is mythological.
Aesop's Fables: animal stories with a moral, by Greek slave and storyteller Aesop. He lived on the island of Samos 2,500 years ago
enquired: asked about something
fared: (here) how her first day went

SUMMARY

Anjali and her parents move to Junagarh. There she meets Pinky, the daughter of Raghuram the gardener, at their mango orchard. The two girls become fast friends. One day, Anjali discovers that Pinky has never gone to school. She doesn't know how to read or write. So, Anjali decides to help Pinky, after her mother, Suman, tells her about the slogan 'Each one, Teach one'. Pinky is eager to learn and Anjali is thrilled with her friend's progress. On Pinky's first day of school, she realizes that she can read, write, and play. Anjali is the happiest person that day.

COMPREHENSION

A. Choose the correct option.

1. Anjali and her parents had shifted
   a. to Junagarh from another city.
   b. from Junagarh to another city.
   c. to Junagarh from Mumbai.
2. Raghuram was
   a. a gardener who worked in a mango orchard.
   b. an officer who worked in a bank.
   c. Pinky's uncle.
3. Anjali introduced Pinky to
   a. the world of animals.
   b. the world of books.
   c. the world of plants.

B. Write T for true and F for false.

1. Anjali's father was the commissioner and her mother worked in a company. ☐
2. Pinky ran away because she did not go to school and felt bad about it. ☐

C. Answer these questions.

1. What was one of the many things that Anjali liked about Junagarh?
2. How did Anjali help Pinky learn to read and write?
3. Do you think Anjali did the right thing by giving her old books to Pinky? Why?
4. How do you think Anjali felt after helping Pinky to learn reading and writing?
5. How do you think Pinky's life changed after Anjali helped her? What would have happened if Anjali had not met Pinky?

Life Skills and Values

Helping others

Anjali was the happiest when Pinky started going to school. Why do we feel happy when we help others? Think of an incident when you helped somebody and felt happy. Narrate the incident in class.

VOCABULARY

Compound words

A **compound word** is a word formed by combining two words. For example:

bed + room = bedroom *foot + ball = football* *lap + top = laptop*

A. Choose words from Column A and match them with those in Column B to form compound words.

Column A	Column B
1. wood	a. bow
2. news	b. cake
3. pan	c. land
4. rain	d. paper
5. up	e. sheet
6. work	f. side

B. Fill in the blanks with the words formed in Ex A.

1. The .... gives us the latest news.
2. There is a beautiful .... in the sky.
3. The .... on grammar was very easy.
4. I visited a .... in my dream last night.
5. My mother baked a delicious .... for me yesterday.
6. Anjali was unable to solve the puzzle because the blocks were placed .... down.

DICTIONARY SKILLS

Circle the correct spelling. You may use a dictionary for help.

1. a. axcited	b. exceted	c. excited
2. a. preised	b. praised	c. praized
3. a. treasure	b. treazure	c. treesure
4. a. fevourite	b. faworite	c. favourite
5. a. magazine	b. magezine	c. magajine

GRAMMAR

Articles

- **Articles** tell us if a noun is singular or plural. They also tell us if the noun is general or specific.
- There are two types of articles—indefinite article and definite article.

Indefinite article

- The indefinite article is *a/an*. It is used when we don't specify the things or the people we are talking about. For example:

  I met a friend.

- The indefinite article is always used with a singular noun when it is used for the first time. For example:

  I saw a cat outside my house.

- The indefinite article *a* is used before consonant sounds. For example:

  The dogs lived in a shelter.

- The indefinite article *an* is used before vowel sounds. For example:

  It is an allergy.

Definite article

- The definite article is *the*. It is used when we talk about a specific person or thing that both the speaker and the listener know. For example:

  The President is visiting the Taj Mahal.

Some rules

- When we speak of someone or something for the first time, we use *a* or *an*. The next time we repeat that noun, we use *the*. For example:

  A boy came in. The boy had a large bag in his hands.

- Do not use articles with names of countries, states, cities, lakes and mountains. For example:

  He lives in Manali. He is training to climb Mount Everest.

- If a country is a collection of states, we use the definite article. For example:

  the United States *the United Kingdom*

- Do not use articles with plurals and uncountable nouns. For example:

  She writes books. *He loves classical music.*

A. Fill in the blanks with suitable articles.

1. The boy bought .... apple-shaped plate.
2. Pinky found .... storybook on the shelf.
3. One day, Anjali noticed .... new hoarding outside her house.
4. He put his cat on the sofa. .... angry cat scratched the sofa.
5. Anjali went on .... safari. .... safari was .... great experience.
6. Mani spotted .... injured dog and took it to the vet.
7. I forgot .... carry-bag at home. I had to walk all .... way back to get it.
8. I bought .... bunch of clothes and .... assortment of things for my house.
9. In order to reach the station on time, I booked .... Uber cab.
10. Naman is so good at solving puzzles that it takes him .... minute to solve .... Rubik's cube.

Prepositions of time

- We use prepositions to describe a relationship between a noun and the other words in a sentence.
- Prepositions used to show time related to the noun are called **prepositions of time.**
- The words *at*, *in*, and *on* are three common prepositions of time.
- *In* is used
  - to talk about years.

    He was born in 1994.
  - to talk about months.

    I visited Delhi in December.
  - to talk about decades.

    The film was released in the seventies.
  - to talk about centuries.

    The machine was invented in the eighteenth century.
  - to talk about seasons.

    We wear warm clothes in winter.

- to talk about periods of time.

  The bridge was built in six months.

- *On* is used
  - to talk about days.

    He returned on Tuesday.
  - to talk about the morning/afternoon/evening/night of a certain day.

    He called me on Monday morning.
  - to talk about dates.

    Independence Day is celebrated on 15 August.
- *At* is used
  - to express an exact time of the clock.

    I have a music class at one o'clock.
  - to talk about holiday periods.

    He will come home at Christmas.
  - with the words *night, sunrise,* and *sunset.*

    Owls hunt at night.
  - to talk about meal times like lunchtime and dinner time.

    The canteen is crowded at lunchtime.

B. Fill in the blanks with suitable prepositions of time.

1. His birthday falls .... 12 May.
2. Where will you go .... Sunday?
3. It rained heavily .... July this year.
4. The supermarket is closed .... night.
5. I will meet my friend .... 11 a.m.
6. Anjali's old books were lying .... the attic.
7. Riya went home .... lunchtime as she was unwell.
8. Did you attend the dance class .... your birthday?
9. The world made great progress .... the twentieth century.
10. Will we be able to travel to Mars .... the twenty-first century?
11. The film Sholay was made .... the seventies but it is still very popular today.
12. New Delhi gets nearly fourteen hours of sunlight .... the summers.
13. Nilli decided that she will take swimming classes .... Mondays and singing lessons .... Thursdays.
14. When one joins the army, one has to wake up every day .... sunrise.
15. Nilima and Parveen planned to meet .... quarter to twelve outside the metro station.

LISTENING AND SPEAKING

Listening

A. Listen to the poem *The Arrow and the Song* by Henry Wadsworth Longfellow and fill in the blanks.

The Arrow and the Song

I shot an .... into the air,
It fell to ...., I knew not where;
For, so swiftly it flew, the ....
Could not .... it in its flight.

I breathed a .... into the air,
It .... to earth, I knew not where;
For who has sight so .... and strong,
That it can follow the .... of song?

Long, long afterward, in an ....
I .... the arrow, still unbroke;
And the ...., from beginning to end,
I found again in the .... of a friend.

Speaking

B. Divide the class into groups of ten. Each team will create a chain story.

21st Century Skills: Communication, Collaboration

Here are the rules for the players:

- Each person can say only one sentence and the story must continue.
- The first player begins the story by saying 'Once there lived a young girl in the city of Mumbai...' and completes the sentence.
- The next player will continue the story in a meaningful way.
- This process continues until it reaches the last player in the team.
- The last player will conclude the story in one sentence.

Choose one of these as the theme of your story.

1. Friendship 2. Sharing 3. Kindness 4. Helping others

WRITING

Chotu, an orphan, works in a tea stall. Write a paragraph on how you would help him so that he can stop working and go to school.

I see him every day.

3 Shadow and Carly

Animal friends

OBJECTIVES

In this chapter, we will:

- *read a story about love for animals and friendship with them.*
- *learn to use friendship terms and idioms.*
- *learn to identify the subject and the predicate.*
- *learn to punctuate sentences.*
- *listen to a story and fill in the blanks.*
- *learn to make requests and respond to requests.*
- *practise writing an informal letter.*

WARM-UP

Mindfulness Activity

Being mindful about other living beings

A. As human beings, we feel many emotions like joy, sadness, anger, surprise, etc. What about animals? Do you think they feel these emotions as well? Discuss your thoughts with a partner.
Look at the pictures. Then, write the emotions you think the animal may feel.

1. .... 2. .... 3. .... 4. .... 5. ....

Observe animals and plants around you. You will notice that in many ways, they can express how they feel. You may note your observations and discuss them in the class.

B. Do you have a pet? Identify the pets shown below and tick the pet you have. If you do not have a pet, tick the one you would like to adopt.

READING

Read this story about how caring and loving cats can be, and what it means to have a home where you are loved and cared for.

Science Scan

- Cats, tigers, lions, jaguars, leopards, and cheetahs all belong to the cat family.
- Pet cats and small wild cats are called *small cats,* while the others are called *big cats.*
- All cats are carnivores.

allergic: caused by or related to an allergy
allergy: extreme sensitivity to a substance, especially a food, pollen, fur, or dust, which causes the body to react to it causing discomfort

'Goodbye, Shadow,' Paige said as her family dropped me off at the cat shelter. 'I know you'll find a good home soon. I'm sorry, I'm allergic to you.' She held me tight and her tears hit my fur. I couldn't bear to see her so sad, so I told myself it was the allergy that made her eyes so wet.

'Always remember that I love you, and I want you to find another special human. The shelter is nice, but a cat needs a *forever home*. A cat needs to *belong* somewhere,' she said.

After she left, my eyes were overflowing somehow. Maybe I was allergic to the other cats. They were everywhere.

A cat sniffed me, then nudged my side. 'Are you okay?' she asked.

'Of course,' I said, backing away.

She looked me straight in the eye, and I knew she understood me. I was embarrassed that she saw me cry.

'I had a cold when I came in too,' she said.

'It's an allergy,' I replied.

'Well, you'll feel better tomorrow and better each day after that. I'm Carly.'

'I'm Shadow.' We touched noses to complete the introduction.

'I'll show you around. I've been here almost two years,' she said.

Two years! I knew I couldn't be without a family for that long.

Carly introduced me to everyone: Isabel, Theo, Scamp.

She said. 'You'll like it in here. We aren't kept in cages and we can stay until we find *forever homes*, even if it takes years.'

I settled in and found a bed next to a cat tree. I felt odd; I was used to sleeping by Paige.

The next morning a boy and his mom came in. The boy petted me, then walked away. I knew he must be filling out the adoption papers. I just imagined hands would pick me up and put me in a carrier, but, the boy picked up Isabel.

Of course, he would want her. She was beautiful. My colours are in odd patterns.

'Congratulations, Isabel! I'll miss you, but I'm happy for you,' I said.

'Maybe we need to groom some more,' I suggested to Carly.

The next morning I groomed until my tongue was as dry as fresh litter. A girl and her dad came in. The girl threw a fur mouse and I pounced on it to prove I was a good mouse catcher. They walked away.

I just knew hands would pick me up and put me in a carrier, but the girl picked up Theo. Of course, she would want him. He was talkative.

embarrassed: felt shy or ashamed
cat tree: an artificial structure made of wood and covered with carpet for cats to play, exercise, and relax on
petted: stroked or patted lovingly
adoption: the action of legally taking up another's child or an animal and bringing it up as one's own
carrier: (here) a basket-like case for transporting small pets
groom: to clean the fur or skin by licking
litter: a material used to line a shallow container which is used by cats as an indoor toilet

Fact File

- There is a saying that *a cat has nine lives.* This is because a cat's collarbones are not attached to any other bones but connected to its shoulders only by muscles. This gives cats great flexibility and freedom of movement. They can squeeze into what seem like small openings and don't get hurt even after falling from heights.
- Cats can also drink seawater and survive droughts. This is because their kidneys can filter seawater and remove the salt content from it!

snuggle: to settle into a warm, comfortable position
jangle: to make or cause to make a ringing metallic sound

'Congratulations, Theo! I'll miss you, but I'm happy for you,' I said.

I made more friends, but lost them when they found homes. Carly was always there to play with me, though.

Every time I think of how much I wanted a home and a special human friend, that old allergy comes back to my eye. Then, I remembered what Paige told me – that someone would adopt me, and Paige never, ever lied to me.

We tried to get adopted. We saw lots of people, but no one chose us. One early spring morning, Carly woke me up with 'Happy Anniversary! You've been my friend for a year.'

She meant to be nice, but I wasn't happy. How had I not found a home in a whole year? I decided to sleep all day.

Around lunchtime a human sat down and put me on her lap. I refused to snuggle.

I heard a carrier door jangle, but I wouldn't look to see which friend was leaving.

'Bye, Shadow! I finally have a home. But I'll really miss you. You're my best friend.'

I couldn't congratulate her. I couldn't say goodbye.

Instead, I did something I'd never done before. I extended my claws and scratched. I scratched the couch, the wallpaper. I scratched everything I could, except a cat or a human. Even when I'm upset, I never hurt anyone.

Someone called my name. I just knew I was in trouble. A pair of hands picked me up and put me in a carrier. At last, I was being adopted.

'He's the cutest, sweetest cat here,' said the girl whose lap I had been on.

'Our other new cat is cute and sweet too,' said the boy. 'I'd say it's a tie.'

They took me to the car and Carly was already there. We were being adopted together! She winked at me. I winked back. And amazingly, we never got 'allergies' again.

SUMMARY

Paige is heartbroken. She is allergic to her beloved cat Shadow and has to drop him off at the cat shelter. When Paige leaves, Shadow is in tears but he thinks it is his allergy to other cats in the shelter. Another cat, Carly, comes and talks to Shadow. She tells him that she had a cold too when she arrived at the shelter. They become friends. They do not find anyone who chooses them for adoption. One year passes by. Shadow grows increasingly sad that he does not have a forever home. He does not wish Carly goodbye when she gets adopted. But luckily, the same family adopts Shadow moments later. He finally has a forever home and his best friend Carly is with him.

COMPREHENSION

A. Choose the correct option.

1. Whose family dropped Shadow off at the shelter?
   a. Carly's family
   b. Paige's family
   c. Theo's family
2. Shadow told himself that it was the
   a. fever that made Paige's eyes wet.
   b. allergy that made Paige's eyes wet.
   c. strong wind that made Paige's eyes wet.
3. Who was Shadow's first friend at the shelter?
   a. Carly
   b. Paige
   c. Theo
4. Who was adopted first?
   a. Isabel
   b. Scamp
   c. Shadow
5. For how long were Shadow and Carly not adopted?
   a. For a fortnight
   b. For a month
   c. For a year

B. Answer the questions.

1. Why did Shadow feel odd after settling in at the cat shelter?
2. Why, according to Shadow, was Theo adopted by the girl?
3. Why was Shadow upset when Carly wished him a happy anniversary?
4. How did Shadow react when Carly was adopted? Why?
5. What happened to Shadow and Carly in the end?
6. What do you think actually caused tears in Paige's eyes when her family dropped off Shadow at the cat shelter?
7. Do you think Shadow is a nice, likeable cat? Give reasons to support your answer.
8. What kind of person did Paige want Shadow to be adopted by? What does that show about Paige?

Life Skills and Values — **Empathy for animals**

1. Paige loved Shadow even though she could not keep him as a pet. It is not possible for everyone to adopt pets. In what other ways, then, can we show our love for animals?
2. Many people abandon their pets on streets when the pets grow old or catch a disease. What would you say to those people?

VOCABULARY

Friendship terms

- Shadow and Carly were *best friends*.
- There are various kinds of friends. For example:
    - best friend: a friend who you are closest to
    - companion: a person with whom you spend a lot of time
    - confidant: a friend whom you trust and share your secrets with
    - mate: your friend with whom you have a lot in common interests
    - acquaintance: someone you know slightly, but who is not a close friend

A. Fill in each blank with the most appropriate term from the ones defined above.

1. Shadow and Carly remained .... forever.
2. Carly was Shadow's .... as she shared all her problems with him.
3. Shadow never knew that he would meet a new .... at the shelter.

4. Shadow and Theo were ....

5. I met an .... after many months.

Idioms

- An idiom is a phrase or group of words whose meaning is different from the meanings of the individual words. Here are some examples of idioms with the word sight:
  - a sorry sight: when someone is not well-presented and it makes you feel pitiful
  - at first sight: when you see something for the first time
  - catch sight of: when you see something or someone just for a moment
  - lose sight of: when something you do not focus on the more important task or situation at hand
  - no end in sight: when you cannot see an end to troubles or work
  - to set your sights on: when you decide to focus or aim on achieving something

B. Fill in each blank with a suitable idiom from the ones given above.

1. Though the offer looks attractive ...., it has too many conditions.
2. As I opened the window, I .... a dove flying over the mountain.
3. The boatman started his journey and soon .... land.
4. The poor man's damaged house is ....
5. To achieve success in life, one should .... the goal.
6. There is .... to the water scarcity problem we have been facing since last month.

GRAMMAR

Subject and Predicate

- The **subject** of a sentence is the person or thing the sentence talks about.

  Cherime loves mangoes.

  Cherime is the subject of the above sentence, as the sentence talks about her.

- The **predicate** is the sentence part that tells us something about the subject. It includes a verb.

  Anjali loves mangoes.

  What does the above sentence tell us about Anjali? It says that she loves mangoes. So, *loves mangoes* is the predicate in the sentence.

  Virat Kohli scored a century in the final match.

  In the above sentence, *Virat Kohli* is the subject and the rest of the sentence is the predicate.

A. Choose a suitable subject from the box and complete each sentence.

A doctor *Her friend* *The tennis player* *My father* *The big spider* *The bumble bee*

1. .... gave her a new pen.
2. .... spun a web above the door.
3. .... sucked nectar from the flower.
4. .... was very happy when I helped him.
5. .... visited our school yesterday for the students' routine check-up.
6. .... injured her shoulder when she smashed the ball hard across the court.

B. Choose a suitable predicate from the box and complete each sentence.

barked all night is a great chess player landed the aircraft safely
fluttered in the wind caused a lot of heat strokes has a long trunk
knows how to say a few words watered the plants regularly

1. The flag ....
2. The dogs ....
3. The pilot ....
4. The gardener ....
5. The elephant ....
6. Magnus Carlsen ....
7. The parrot ....
8. The heat wave in central India ....

Punctuation

- We use certain marks or signs in writing to make our meaning clear. These marks are called **punctuation marks.**
- The **comma (,)**, the **full stop (.)**, the **question mark (?)** and the **exclamation mark (!)** are some common punctuation marks.
- The system of using punctuation marks is called **punctuation.**
- The comma is used to separate items in a list. For example:

  I bought apples, grapes, guavas and *strawberries.*
- The comma is also used after the word that refers to the listener. For example:

  Uncle, where are you going?

  This is for you, Lina.
- The full stop is used at the end of a sentence that tells us something. For example:

  I have a toy car.

Navit lives in Delhi.

- The question mark is used at the end of a sentence that asks a question. For example:

    When are you leaving for Shillong?

    Are Sangita and Mukul studying?

- The exclamation mark is used at the end of a sentence that expresses a strong or sudden feeling like happiness, pain, fear, surprise, etc. For example:

    How beautiful the stars look!

    Ouch! I stubbed my toe on the door stopper.

- Each sentence begins with a capital letter. For example:

    Tigers hunt at night.

C. The passage has errors in each line. Rewrite it correctly by using punctuation marks and capital letters appropriately.

once a mother goat and her kid lived ....

in a cave in a jungle? one day an elephant ....

passed by their cave, The kid was afraid ....

to see the elephant. it said, 'how big that animal is ....

It will eat us alive. What shall we do Should we get ....

out and run away.' The mother goat said, 'Relax ....

elephants don't eat meat. they eat green leaves ....

grass sugarcane and fruits.' ....

....

....

LISTENING AND SPEAKING

Listening

A. Listen to what happens to Shadow and Carly after they are adopted and fill in the blanks.

1. Shadow and Carly were adopted by Jenny and her ...., Jim.
2. They lived in a .... near the sea.
3. They went to the .... every evening and played there.
4. Jenny took care of .... and Jim took care of ....
5. Sleeping by ...., Shadow often remembered ....

Speaking

Communication Collaboration

Making a request

- It's important to be polite when you ask people for something or request them to do something for you.
- You can make a request using the following sentence structures.

  Can you please ...?

  Could you please ...?

  Will you please ...?

  Would you mind ...?

  Could you/Can you/Would you/Will you please open the door for me?

  Would you mind opening the door for me?

Things to remember

- *Could* is more polite than *can*.
- Use the word *please* to make your request polite.

Responding to a request

- Here are some of the ways in which you can respond to a request.

Positive Response	Negative Response
Yes, of course. *With pleasure.* *Sure, here you are.*	*I'm sorry I can't.* *I'm afraid I can't.* *I'm sorry, I need it myself.*

B. Work in pairs. Make suitable requests for the given situations. Your partner will respond to the requests appropriately. Perform the activity taking turns.

1. You want to borrow your partner's pencil.
2. You need your partner's notebook to complete your schoolwork.
3. Your partner is going to a stationery store. You need to buy a ruler.
4. You are thirsty. Ask your partner for a glass of water.
5. You need a sheet of paper. You want to borrow it from your partner.
6. The window is shut and it is hot in the room. Request your partner to open the window, since he/she is standing near it.

WRITING

Creative Thinking Imagination

Imagine you are Paige. Write a letter to Shadow's new parents. Mention how you miss Shadow and how happy you are to hear that he has found a home with two loving and caring children.

4 The Fox's Wedding

Animal friends

OBJECTIVES

In this chapter, we will:

- *read a poem based on a folklore.*
- *learn to use cardinal and ordinal numbers.*
- *learn to make wind chimes.*

WARM-UP

Mindfulness Activity
The importance of gratitude

Work in pairs and discuss with your partner.

1. Form a circle. Take a minute to think about what you are grateful for. It could be a simple hug from your mother, a smile from your friend or a pretty bird that you saw on the way to school. Write this on a piece of paper and share it with the person on your left.
2. Do you remember getting a special gift ever? Draw the gift on the space given below and write what made it special? Show it to the class.

3. When a story or belief is passed through the generations by word of mouth, it becomes a folklore. Discuss any one folklore from your region.

READING

There is a common folklore in the Indian subcontinent, many African countries, Brazil, France and Japan that when the sun shines during the rain, a fox gets married. Let's read this folk poem by Harindranath Chattopadhyay about a fox's wedding and find out who all attend it.

The cloud is dropping
It rain in the sun,
For the Fox's wedding
Has just begun.

From forest and plain
And mountainside,
Guests bring gifts
For the Fox and the bride.

Here comes the first:
A grinning hyena,
Who brings a charming
Bowl from China.

Here comes the second:
A lion bold,
Whose gift is a mirror
Of African gold.

Here comes the third:
A crocodile,
Whose gift is a silver
Cup from the Nile.

Here comes the fourth:
A long-necked camel,
Whose gift is a casket
Of Indian enamel.

grinning: smiling broadly
casket: a small box or chest for keeping jewels, letters, or valued objects
enamel: a glossy substance applied on metallic or hard surfaces as a protective coating

Here comes the fifth:
A monkey who writes,
His gift is a book,
The Arabian Nights.

Here comes the sixth:
A she-wolf **vain**,
Who brings for the bride
A scarf from Spain.

Here comes the seventh:
A polar bear,
Whose gift is a beautiful
Russian chair.

Here comes the eighth
To the Fox's marriage:
A horse who has brought him
A five-wheeled carriage.

Here comes the ninth:
A jackal who brings
The bride and the bridegroom
Two diamond rings.

Here comes the tenth:
If you please, uninvited;
The guests at the wedding
Are getting excited.

He comes from somewhere
And teaches **zoology**.
What is his gift?
An **empty apology**.

vain: arrogant; extremely proud
zoology: the science of animal life
empty apology: saying sorry without meaning it

But why has he come
To the Fox's feast?
It is most ill-mannered
To say the least.

The Fox then addressed
The guests who were present:
'Let us be friendly,
Let us be pleasant.

'Let us be civil
And not make a fuss
Since Man, after all,
Is a beast like us.'

The guests of a sudden,
Ceased to complain;
The clouds of a sudden,
Forgot to rain.

The sun came out
Both gay and splendid;
The Fox's wedding
Was happily ended.

ceased: stopped
splendid: wonderful

SUMMARY

The poem describes a fox's wedding and all the guests who attended it. The guests include a hyena, a lion, a crocodile, a camel, a monkey, a she-wolf, a polar bear, a horse and a jackal. All the guests bring beautiful gifts. Only the man being comes as an uninvited guest and does not bring a gift. The other guests notice this and begin to complain. However, the fox requests the guests to forgive the man and treat him well. Finally, the rain stops, and the sun comes out. The wedding ends happily.

COMPREHENSION

A. Choose the correct option.

1. The guests had gathered to attend
   a. the hyena's wedding.
   b. the crocodile's wedding.
   c. the Fox's wedding.
2. It started raining
   a. before the wedding ceremony began.
   b. just after the wedding ceremony began.
   c. after the wedding ceremony was over.
3. The lion brought as a gift
   a. a bowl made of African gold.
   b. a plate made of African gold.
   c. a mirror made of African gold.
4. The eighth guest was
   a. a horse.
   b. a monkey.
   c. a she-wolf.
5. The uninvited guest was
   a. a bird.
   b. a snake.
   c. a man.

B. Answer these questions.

1. How many guests attended the Fox's wedding?
2. Who was the fifth guest? What did he bring?
3. Who was the long-necked guest? What did he bring?
4. Can you guess what the Nile is? Which gift was brought from there?
5. What did the Fox say to the other guests about the uninvited guest?

Life Skills and Values — **Courtesy**

1. How would you have behaved with the uninvited guest if you were in place of the Fox?
2. Going to a party without an invitation is considered rude and impolite. Have you ever gone to a birthday party without being invited?

Cardinal and ordinal numbers

- Numbers like *one, two,* and *three* are called **cardinal numbers**. Cardinal numbers do not show the order or position. They just mention the number of people or things. For example:

  Do you have two pens?

  There are seven notebooks on the table.

- Numbers like *first, second,* and *third* are called **ordinal numbers**. Ordinal numbers express the order or position of something in a series. For example:

  The hyena was the first to arrive.

  The seventh to arrive was the polar bear.

A. Here is the list of the animals that attended the Fox's wedding. However, their order is jumbled. Write the order of their arrival, using ordinal numbers, in the blank.

1. camel ....
2. crocodile ....
3. horse ....
4. hyena ....
5. jackal ....
6. lion ....
7. polar bear ....
8. she-wolf ....

B. There is a mistake of cardinal and ordinal numbers in each sentence. Correct and rewrite the sentences. Also, say whether the numbers in your new sentences are ordinal or cardinal.

1. The three chair from the left is broken.

   .... (ordinal/cardinal)

2. There are twentieth benches in the classroom.

   .... (ordinal/cardinal)

3. Tom was so hungry that he ate fifth sandwiches.

   .... (ordinal/cardinal)

4. I won the one position in the painting competition.

   .... (ordinal/cardinal)

5. Zeenat was sitting in the two row at the magic show.

   .... (ordinal/cardinal)

ACTIVITY

Do you like giving and receiving gifts? Follow the instructions and make a simple wind chime, which you can then gift to a family member or a friend.

Things required

- a stick
- simple strings
- old spoons or metal scraps
- oil pastel paint

Procedure

- Take a stick. You may paint it if you wish.
- Take a few old metal spoons or metal scraps from the nearest junkyard or recycling workshop. Paint them in different colours with oil pastels. You may use the pastel paints that are organically made.
- String the spoons or the scraps on a string. Then, tie four or five such strings to the stick. Your wind chime is complete.
- Hang the wind chime on a tree, on a windowsill, or simply on a pole. Listen to its sound or 'chime' when it moves in the breeze.
- You can make more wind chimes like this with different materials and listen to the different sounds they make.

Picture story

5 The Samurai Warrior and the Tea Master

Finding solutions

OBJECTIVES

In this chapter, we will:

- *read a story about overcoming difficulties.*
- *learn adjective-noun collocations.*
- *learn to use subjective, objective and reflexive pronouns.*
- *listen to a description of Ninja warriors and mark sentences as true or false.*
- *learn to spot and describe differences between the given pictures.*
- *learn the different sounds of ough.*
- *practise writing a recipe.*

WARM-UP

Mindfulness Activity

Appreciating our food

A. Eating and drinking is something that we all do every day. Let's play a Tasting Game with your partner.

Steps:

1. Bring an assortment of dried fruits and nuts.
2. Close your eyes. Take a piece of a dried food or a nut and smell it.
3. Then, nibble it. Do not chew it. Feel and taste it first.
4. Chew it slowly, savoring the taste and texture of the food.
5. Guess the name of the thing you ate. Your partner will tell you if you guessed it right or not.
6. Repeat the exercise, with your partner tasting the food this time.

This will help you to enjoy the food that you eat. You can try it even with the things you drink. You will also learn to appreciate your food in a better way.

B. Look at the picture clues and fill in the blanks.

bullet train

kimono

Mount Fuji

samurai

Kendo

sushi

1. .... is Japan's highest mountain.
2. .... is a popular Japanese rice dish.
3. Japan's high speed train is called the ....
4. The .... were traditional Japanese military soldiers.
5. The .... is the traditional dress worn by Japanese women.
6. .... is a Japanese form of fencing with bamboo swords, originally developed as a safe form of sword training for samurai.

READING

Many centuries ago in Japan, there was a warrior community known as the samurai. *The* samurai *were the master of their mind and body, and skilful swordsmen. Read this story of one such samurai, Lord Yamanouchi.*

Lord Yamanouchi was a wise man and a respectable lord at the emperor's court. A tea master worked in the service of Lord Yamanouchi.

The Japanese tea ceremony is a graceful ritual of preparing green tea. The utensils, the sitting arrangement for both the guests and the host, the steps of preparing, serving, and drinking tea are all predefined.

Once, Lord Yamanouchi and the tea master went on business to the great city of Edo. One evening, the tea master and his friends were taking a stroll.

ceremony: a formal and traditional occasion, one celebrating an event
ritual: a serious ceremony that consists of a series of actions performed as per a prescribed order
predefined: defined or established in advance

Suddenly, they came face to face with a samurai warrior. The tea master stepped into the drain on the side to let him pass.

imposter: a person who is pretending to be someone else in order to trick people
duel: a formal fight with weapons between two people to settle a point of honour
robes: long loose outer garments reaching to the ankles

At Lord Yamanouchi's palace...

confident: feeling sure about one's abilities

SUMMARY

Lord Yamanouchi is a samurai warrior. A tea master works for him. The tea master prepares tea skillfully. Impressed with him, Lord Yamanouchi gives the tea master the rank and title of a samurai warrior. The tea master meets another samurai warrior who challenges him to a duel. The tea master decides to accept the challenge and requests Lord Yamanouchi to teach him to fight. Lord Yamanouchi agrees and advises him to face the samurai warrior with confidence and peace of mind. The tea master follows his advice. His confidence wins the samurai warrior over. The samurai warrior seeks the tea master's forgiveness and refuses to fight with him.

COMPREHENSION

A. Choose the correct option.

1. Who was Lord Yamanouchi?
   a. A king
   b. A samurai warrior
   c. A poor tea master
2. Which city did Lord Yamanouchi and the tea master visit?
   a. Edo
   b. India
   c. Japan
3. What did the samurai warrior want?
   a. A gift from the tea master
   b. A duel with the tea master
   c. A gold coin from the tea master
4. What was the tea master very good at?
   a. Riding a horse
   b. Fighting with a sword
   c. Performing the tea ceremony

B. Answer the questions.

1. Why did Lord Yamanouchi give the tea master the rank of a samurai warrior?
2. What happened in the city of Edo?
3. What advice did the tea master's friends give him?
4. How was the tea master able to defend himself against the samurai warrior?
5. Do you think the tea master was a man of courage and self-esteem? Give reasons to support your answer.
6. Why do you think Lord Yamanouchi advised the tea master to maintain peace of mind?

Life Skills and Values

Focusing on goals

1. Do you think it was the tea master's quality of focusing on his goal that helped him achieve great success in life? Explain.
2. Imagine you have an exam tomorrow. Your father is watching the final of an important cricket tournament on television and you are tempted to join him. What would you do in that situation? Why?

VOCABULARY

Collocations: adjectives and nouns

- A **collocation** is two or more words that are frequently used together. For example:

  This is strong coffee.

  Here *strong coffee* is a **collocation**.

  However, we cannot say 'powerful coffee', even if 'strong' and 'powerful' mean the same thing. We need to know which words will work together to make the word combinations sound correct.

- There are several different word combinations that can make up a collocation. *Strong coffee* is an example of an **adjective + noun collocation**. Some more examples of adjective + noun collocations are: *fierce duel* *foul smell*

Circle the correct adjectives to form correct collocations. The nouns are the words in bold.

1. He has a *rich/high* **vocabulary**.
2. The samurai were *forceful/powerful* **warriors**.
3. A mother has *deep/high* **love** for her children.
4. The noise of *loud/heavy* **traffic** can give you a headache.
5. He spoke with a *heavy/strong* **American accent**.
6. I took the *express/quick* **train** to the airport to save time.

GRAMMAR

Pronouns

- A **pronoun** is a word used in place of a noun that has already been mentioned once. This is done to avoid repeating the noun. For example:

  Payal was tired, so she went to bed.

- **Personal pronouns** are used in place of nouns referring to specific people or things. For example, *I*, *me*, *you*, *yours*, *her*, *we*, *they*, and *them* are personal pronouns. These pronouns are divided into different categories according to their usage and role in a sentence.

Subjective pronouns

- The pronouns **I, you, he, she, we, it,** and **they** are known as **subjective pronouns** because they act as the subjects of verbs or subjects of sentences. For example:

  I waved at her.

  We drove Vicky home.

  She saw Payal walking towards the market.

Objective pronouns

- The pronouns me, you, us, him, her, it, and them are known as **objective pronouns** because they act as the objects of verbs and prepositions. For example:

  She waved at me.

  Vicky drove us home.

  Paige saw her.

- Here's a table of different forms of pronouns for your easy reference:

	SINGULAR		PLURAL	
	Subjective	**Objective**	**Subjective**	**Objective**
first person	I	me	we	us
second person	you	you	you	you
third person	he/she/it	him/her/it	they	them

- Notice that the pronouns you and it stay the same, whether used in the subjective or objective roles.

Reflexive Pronouns

- A **reflexive pronoun** refers back to the subject of the sentence. Myself, himself, herself, itself, yourself, yourselves, ourselves and themselves are reflexive pronouns. For example:

  He hurt himself while playing volleyball.

  I don't like to praise myself.

  She is preparing herself for the long journey.

Fill in each blank with the correct pronoun.

1. Why are .... crying, Amit?
2. .... have submitted our notebooks.
3. I know that boy, ... is my neighbour.
4. Raman is absent because .... has a fever.
5. Look at the flowers. How beautiful .... look!
6. She did not attend the phone but I have sent .... a message.
7. He looked at .... in the mirror after putting on his new shirt.
8. The king loved his daughter very much. He never scolded ....

LISTENING AND SPEAKING

Listening

A. Listen to a description of ninja warriors. Then mark the statements as true (T) or false (F).

1. Ninja warriors lived in China 200 years ago. ☐
2. Ninjas were not only fighters, they were spies too. ☐
3. Ninjas worked for themselves. ☐
4. Their main weapon was a sword. ☐
5. A ninja usually wore white clothes. ☐
6. Japanese people believe that ninjas had magical powers. ☐

Speaking

21st Century Skills: Critical Thinking, Collaboration

B. Work in pairs. Spot the differences between the two pictures. Then, describe the differences to your partner.

Picture A

Picture B

Pronunciation

C. Look at the table below and find out the eight ways to say words with 'ough'.

like *o* in go	like *oo* in too	like *off* in offer	like *uff* in suffer	like *ow* in flower	like *aw* in saw	like *a* in above	like **up** in **up**
th**ough**	thr**ough**	c**ough**	r**ough**	pl**ough**	b**ough**t	bor**ough**	hicc**ough**
alth**ough**		tr**ough**	t**ough**	dr**ough**t	f**ough**t	thor**ough**	
d**ough**			en**ough**		th**ough**t	thor**ough**fare	
d**ough**nut					**ough**t		

D. Fill in each blank with the correct word from the table above. Read out the sentences aloud with the correct pronunciation.

1. We need .... to bake a cake.
2. He needs a medicine for his ....
3. I do not have .... money to buy a cycle.
4. The farmer uses his .... in the field.
5. The samurai warrior was a .... person.

WRITING

Find out how to make lemon ice tea and write down the recipe in simple steps. You can also draw or paste a picture for each step on a separate sheet of paper or a chart paper.

PROJECT 1

UNDERSTANDING OUR CULTURE THROUGH CELEBRATIONS

Traditional ceremonies and celebrations are important aspects of all cultures.

In India, every community has its unique festival and celebration. These special occasions help us bond with one another. These are traditions that are passed on to the next generation.

Speak to your parents about any one ceremony that is held in your family or community. Write about the ceremony in your scrap book or prepare a PowerPoint presentation. Include the following points in your presentation.

- The name of the ceremony/celebration
- The festival or occasion when it is organized
- Preparations made
- Guests invited
- Details of the ceremony being performed
- A special feast which is prepared
- The clothes worn and the songs/dances (if any) that are a part of the celebration

Paste pictures of the ceremony being performed to make your presentation colourful.

6 Earnestness

Focusing on goals

OBJECTIVES

In this chapter, we will:

- *read and understand a poem on the importance of being sincere at one's work.*
- *learn about the literary device, rhyme scheme.*
- *describe our goals through pictures and writing.*

WARM-UP

Mindfulness Activity

Putting thought into our actions

Imagine that you are waiting for your school bus with the rest of your class. When the bus arrives, what do you do? Work in pairs and discuss it. Then choose the option(s) which you think is correct.

- ☐ You decide to rush to board the bus like everyone else.
- ☐ You take charge and organise everyone into a queue.
- ☐ You seek the help of your teacher to ensure that no one rushes to board the bus.
- ☐ You stand at the front, ready to board the bus no matter what.
- ☐ You decide you will help make a queue but stand in the front to get a seat.
- ☐ You wait for everyone else to board the bus and then board it yourself.

READING

Read this poem by Ella Wheeler Wilcox to understand why it is important to put in sincere effort to whatever we do in life.

The hurry of the times affects us so
In this swift rushing hour, we crowd, and press,
And thrust each other backward, as we go,
And do not pause to lay sufficient stress
Upon that good, strong, true word, Earnestness.
In our impetuous haste, could we but know
Its full, deep meaning, its vast import, oh,
Then might we grasp the secret of success!

In that receding age when men were great,
The bone, and sinew, of their purpose lay
In this one word. God likes an earnest soul—
Too earnest to be eager. Soon or late
It leaves the spent horde breathless by the way,
And stands serene, triumphant, at the goal.

swift: (here) passing quickly
press: (here) push forward, without thought
thrust: push forcefully
sufficient: with enough importance
impetuous: to act quickly or suddenly without thinking
haste: (here) the state or quality of doing something too quickly
import: importance
grasp: (here) to understand
receding age: (here) the time that has gone past; olden days
sinew: muscle
spent horde: a crowd of people that is exhausted
serene: calm
triumphant: victorious

SUMMARY

In this poem, the poet tells us the importance of acting with sincerity. She tells us that time makes us hurry, and we are always in a race to finish a work or achieve something. But we need to lay importance on the word *earnestness*. She goes on to say that the true winner is a person who is slow but steady, doing each work with earnest spirit. She even says that she believes that God, too, likes an earnest soul above the rest.

COMPREHENSION

A. Fill in the blanks with words from the box to complete the paragraph.

breathless	*fast-paced*	*sincere*	*earnestness*	*olden days*
honest	*triumphant*	*successful*		

Today, the world is .... and everyone wants to be .... quickly. We push others back in order to move forward in life. In our haste, we fail to understand the importance of .... effort. In the ...., people believed in .... hard work. In our mad rush, we are soon .... and tired, having gained nothing. It is only people who acted with .... that are truly .... at the end.

B. Choose the correct option.

1. Earnestness means
   a. eagerness.
   b. speed.
   c. efficiency.
2. As we go about in this world, we
   a. push others back to go ahead.
   b. wait for our turn to move forward.
   c. we do not care for other's success.
3. In the poem, 'impetuous haste' means
   a. important moment.
   b. to move quickly without thinking.
   c. to move slowly and gracefully.
4. Earlier, truly great people believed in
   a. making an earnest effort in their work.
   b. making lots of money.
   c. succeeding fast.
5. In the poem, 'spent horde' means
   a. an exhausted crowd of people.
   b. money being spent by a horde of people.
   c. a group of people who are sincere.

C. Answer the questions briefly.

1. What does the phrase 'hurry of the times' mean? How does it affect us?
2. What do we not put a lot of importance on?
3. How can we 'grasp the secret of success'?
4. What is the difference between people in the 'receding age' and now?
5. Explain the line 'Too earnest to be eager'. Write about the theme of the poem.

Life Skills and Values — Focusing on goals

1. What would you do if you were not scoring well in a subject repeatedly, even after trying your best?
2. What do you think earnest hard work requires? Discuss with your partner and write down five points.
3. Is it possible for a child of your age to be earnest and sincere? In what ways can you be so?

VOCABULARY

Literary device: Rhyme scheme

In the poem *Earnestness*, every other line ends with a rhyming word. To find out the rhyme scheme of a poem, we can add a letter at the end of the lines with similar rhyming words.

The hurry of the times affects us so A
In this swift rushing hour, we crowd, and press, B
And thrust each other backward, as we go, A
And do not pause to lay sufficient stress B

A. Now, go back to the poem and write the rhyme scheme of its stanzas.

Stanza 1: .... **Stanza 2:** ....

B. Read this poem by R. L. Stevenson. Write the letters in the blanks, and the full rhyme scheme at the bottom.

Faster than fairies, faster than witches, ...
Bridges and houses, hedges and ditches; ....
And charging along like troops in a battle ....
All through the meadows the horses and cattle: ....

All of the sights of the hill and the plain ....
Fly as thick as driving rain; ....
And ever again, in the wink of an eye, ...
Painted stations whistle by. ....

Here is a child who clambers and scrambles, ...
All by himself and gathering brambles; ....
Here is a tramp who stands and gazes; ....
And here is the green for stringing the daisies! ....

Here is a cart runaway in the road ....
Lumping along with man and load; ....
And here is a mill, and there is a river: ....
Each a glimpse and gone forever! ....

Full rhyme scheme: ....

ACTIVITY

21st Century Skills — Critical Thinking

Have you ever dreamt of achieving something big—maybe doing well in academics, sports, or extra-curricular activities? How would you like to achieve that dream—through speed or patience?

Express your goal through pictures and writing.

Draw at least four pictures to show how you will achieve your goal. Each picture should show a stage in your journey to your goal. Give a caption to each picture saying what it shows.

Folk tale

7 The Will

Finding solutions

OBJECTIVES

In this chapter, we will:

- *read a story about the division of camels among three brothers and their mother.*
- *learn to use prefixes and form antonyms of words.*
- *learn to use the same word as a noun and as a verb.*
- *learn to form and use comparative adjectives.*
- *listen to railway announcements and fill in a table.*
- *learn to make suggestions.*
- *practise writing a character sketch.*

WARM-UP

Mindfulness Activity

The importance of sharing

Imagine you were in a picnic and everyone brought the same kind of food. Do you think you will enjoy that get-together? Discuss your thoughts with your partner.

Now draw the various things that you would like to eat in a picnic or a party.

READING

Critical Thinking

How can you divide seventeen camels into two equal halves? Read this Arabian folktale to find out whether that is possible.

Many years ago, in a small town in Egypt, there lived a man named Abdullah bin Saad. Abdullah worked with camels. He had the most **pedigreed** camels of the finest quality with fur as white as a rabbit's. Abdullah loved his camels like his own children.

Once a year, he would sell some of them at a cattle fair and earn a good sum of money. Then he would **rear** the new and the remaining camels and increase his herd.

Abdullah had a good, honest wife and three sons, who lived happily with him in his hut. The camel **enclosure** was right outside the hut. It was a sight to see his handsome camels chewing their **cud** under the leafy date trees in the enclosure.

As time passed, Abdullah and his wife grew weak and old.

One night over dinner, Abdullah bin Saad said to his three sons, 'My boys, I am getting old now and my body is getting weaker every day. I'm sick so often; I feel my end is near. When I'm gone, look after your mother, and please don't fight amongst yourselves. I don't have much, but I have written a **will**, which you can find in a pot in the **granary**.'

One morning soon after, Abdullah was found lifeless in his bed by his wife and sons. Three days after Abdullah's death, his family thought of his will. His sons searched every pot in the granary and finally found a paper wrapped in camel skin. On opening the seal, they found that it was not a will but a **directive** which was addressed to them.

'My children, I ask that the three of you look after your mother. Tell her about your decisions; if you travel anywhere, inform

pedigreed: A pedigreed animal is descended from animals that have all been of a particular type, and is therefore considered to be of good quality.
rear: to care for an animal's young ones until they are fully grown
enclosure: an area that is closed off with a fence
cud: partly digested food returned from the stomach of camels (as well as cattle, sheep, antelopes, deer, and giraffes) to the mouth for further chewing
will: a legal document containing instructions as to what should be done with one's money and property after one's death
granary: a building used for storing grain
directive: an official instruction given by somebody in authority

her before leaving. Ahmad, you are the eldest, so you will have the most responsibility. You must take care of your younger brothers, Muhammad and Mukarram. Ahmad, as the eldest, you must be present for any wedding, death, or any other event in the house. Muhammad, since you are in the middle, you must respect your elder brother and indulge your younger one. You should also respect and love your mother. Mukarram, you are the youngest and the closest to your mother, so you must ensure that every need of your mother's is fulfilled either by you or by your brothers. You must respect your brothers because after me, they will be your elders.'

The sons read the page from top to bottom and looked at each other, horrified that their father had left not a will, but a piece of advice for them.

Then, Rukaiya, Abdullah's wife, said that she remembered that her husband had written on two sheets of paper that night, but they had read only one.

She told them to check if the second page was stuck to the first one. When Ahmad rubbed the corner of the paper, he found that there really was another paper stuck to the first one. The sons' faces lit up. Ahmad said, 'Thank God! Abba has written his will on this one!' Muhammad and Mukarram said, 'Read it quickly, quickly!'

Ahmad began to read.

responsibility: a moral duty that one is required to do, such as take care of someone or something
indulge: to let someone have or do what they want
ensure: to make sure or certain that something happens

Maths Magic

- Numbers like one-half, one-third, and one-ninth are called fractions.

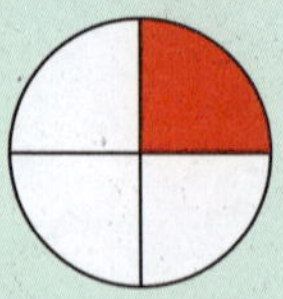

- A fraction is a number that represents the division of a whole number into parts. For example, if you have a pizza and you cut it into 4 equal slices, one of those slices is expressed as one-fourth or $1/4$.
- The shaded area in the diagram represents 1 of the 4 slices of the pizza. It is written as $1/4$.
- A fraction can also represent a part of a group. For example, if you have 5 candies and you give 2 candies to your friend, the division is expressed as $2/5$.

The shaded area represents 2 of the 5 candies. It is expressed as $2/5$.

'With Allah as my witness, I write that after my death, my house goes to my wife, Rukaiya Khatoon. It is up to her to keep it, give it to our sons, or sell it. The decision rests with my wife.

'Apart from my house, I have no other property. However, after my death, my camels will be divided between my wife and children. The healthiest and most handsome camel will go to my wife. The remainder will be divided among my sons. Ahmad will get half of the remaining camels after my wife has taken one. Muhammad will get one-third of the camels and Mukarram will get one ninth.'

Abdullah bin Saad had eighteen camels when he died.
The best camel would go to Rukaiya Khatoon. There remained seventeen beasts.

Ahmad demanded his half, but he could not have half of seventeen camels, which is eight and a half camels. No one knew where to get half a camel. Similarly, when Muhammad asked for one-third and Mukarram for one-ninth, it proved impossible to divide the camels. The three brothers began quarrelling, each wanting his entire share of the animals. None of them was willing to back down.

Their mother exclaimed that their father was hardly buried, and they were already enemies with each other.

Mukkaram, the youngest son, saw that their fighting had made his mother sad. He thought of his father's advice. 'Ammi, you are wise. Why don't you tell us what we should do?' he said.

Remembering his father's advice, Muhammad decided to indulge his younger brother. 'Yes, Ammi, what do you suggest?'

Ahmad, too, realised that his father would want him to respect his mother's wish first. 'Tell us, Ammi, what is your wish?' he asked.

The mother thought for some time. Then she said, 'Let me add my camel to your camels. So how many camels do you have now?

'Eighteen,' said the boys. Ammi said, 'Absolutely correct. Ahmad, you are the eldest, and according to the will you are given half the camels. You get nine of them. Muhammad, according to the will, you get one-third of the camels. One-third of eighteen is six. And Mukarram, according to your father's will, you are given one-ninth of the camels. One-ninth of eighteen is two camels.'

Ammi said that the matter was now settled. Ahmad said, 'Yes, Ammi. I get nine, Muhammad gets six and Mukarram gets two. My God! Together these come to seventeen camels, so your camel will stay with you!' Ammi smiled. She said, 'Your father was a just and honest man.'

just: fair or right

SUMMARY

Abdullah bin Saad lived with his wife Rukaiya Khatoon and three sons: Ahmad, the eldest, Muhammad the middle one and Mukarram the youngest. Abdullah worked with camels. After his death, he left a will dividing his camels and his home among his family. His wife was to get the house and the healthiest camel. He had eighteen camels in all. The sons began to fight as they were unable to divide the seventeen camels as per their father's will. They began to fight among themselves. Rukaiya Khatoon added her camel and sorted the problem. Thus, the matter was resolved.

COMPREHENSION

A. Choose the correct option.

1. Where did Abdullah bin Saad live?
   a. Syria
   b. Egypt
   c. Saudi Arabia
2. When did Abdullah's family start looking for Abdullah's will?
   a. Three days after his death
   b. Two days after his death
   c. A week after his death
3. How many camels did Abdullah leave behind him?
   a. Ten
   b. Nine
   c. Eighteen

4. Who read Abdullah's will?
   a. Ahmad
   b. Mukarram
   c. Rukaiya Khatoon
5. Who was Abdullah's youngest son?
   a. Ahmad
   b. Mukarram
   c. Muhammad

B. Mark the sentences as true (T) or false (F).

1. Abdullah had the finest pedigreed camels. ☐
2. Abdullah loved his camels like his own children. ☐
3. Abdullah's will was kept in the camel enclosure. ☐
4. Mukarram was the eldest son of Abdullah. ☐
5. Abdullah gave his sons bad advice in his will. ☐
6. Ahmad was to receive one-ninth of the camels. ☐

C. Answer these questions.

1. Who was Abdullah bin Saad?
2. How did Abdullah divide his camels in his will?
3. Why did the sons begin to quarrel after reading Abdullah's will?
4. What did Rukaiya Khatoon do to solve the problem?
5. What does Abdullah's will tell you about his nature?
6. Do you like the way Abdullah wrote his will? Give reasons to support your answer.
7. Do you think the three brothers were justified in quarrelling over the division of the camels? Give reasons for your answer.

Life Skills and Values

Sharing with family

1. It is natural to sometimes disagree with one's family or friends. How should we behave when we do not like what someone says or does? How should we solve quarrels?
2. Do you like to share your things with others? What are the things you find easier to share than others?
   How does it feel when you are asked to share your favourite things?
3. Reflect: Do we only share things, possessions and objects? What else do we share? Think of nature, your parents, your teachers, all the people who help you.

VOCABULARY

Prefixes

- A **prefix** is a letter or group of letters added to the beginning of a word to make a new word. For example, when we add the prefix *un-* to the word *happy*, we get *unhappy*.
- Some more examples of prefixes are: *multi-*, *pre-*, *re-*, *semi-*, and *sub-*

  multinational *predefine* *return* *semiconscious* *subtitle*

Antonyms

- An **antonym** is a word that means the opposite of another word. For example, *happy* is the antonym of *sad*.
- Prefixes can be used to create antonyms. For example, *unhappy* is the opposite of *happy*.
- Some negative prefixes used to create antonyms are *dis-*, *il-*, *im-*, and *un-*.

  dishonest *illegal* *impossible* *unfair*

Add an appropriate negative prefix to each word.

1. .... activate
2. .... comfort
3. .... fit
4. .... just
5. .... justice
6. .... match
7. .... motivate
8. .... perfect
9. .... reliable
10. .... spell

DICTIONARY SKILLS

Write the meaning of the new words created in the vocabulary exercise. You can use a dictionary.

1. .... : ....
   ....
2. .... : ....
   ....
3. .... : ....
   ....
4. .... : ....
   ....
5. .... : ....
   ....

6. .... : ....

....

7. .... : ....

....

8. .... : ....

....

9. .... : ....

....

10. .... : ....

....

GRAMMAR

Words used as nouns and verbs

- Many words are used as both nouns and verbs in English.
- Nouns name persons, animals, places, and things. But they can also name feelings such as *love*.
- Verbs describe actions. We use verbs to describe what the nouns do. For example:

  Monkeys eat bananas. Monkeys love bananas.

  Eat and *love* are verbs in these sentences. The word *love* can be both a noun and a verb. For example:

  A mother's love for her child is unconditional.

- There are many words that can be used to name a person, animal, place, or thing and also to describe an action. For example:

  If you are thirsty, you drink (verb) *a drink* (noun).

  He has a sharp mind. (noun)

  Please don't mind the interruption. (verb)

  Her aim is to win the tournament. (noun)

  We should aim high. (verb)

A. Fill in the blanks with suitable words from the box. Then, tick the correct option in the brackets.

book *colour* *walk* *water*

1. I love to draw and .... (noun/verb)
2. Have you read this .... ? (noun/verb)
3. What .... is your new shirt? (noun/verb)
4. I .... in the park every morning. (noun/verb)

5. Please bring me a glass of .... (noun/verb)
6. Did you .... the plants yesterday? (noun/verb)
7. Do you take a .... in the morning? (noun/verb)
8. I will .... a table at the nearest restaurant for dinner. (noun/verb)

Comparative adjectives

- **Adjectives** are words that describe nouns or pronouns.
- The **comparative form of an adjective** is used for comparing two people or things.
- It is used to show the quality of one noun when compared to the other. For example:

  Mukkaram is younger than Ahmad.
- To form the comparative degree of an adjective, *-er* is added to it. For example:

  deep+er = deeper

  great+er = greater

  sweet+er = sweeter
- When we add *-er* to adjectives, the last consonant is sometimes doubled. For example:

  fat+er = fatter

  hot+er = hotter
- The comparative degree of a few adjectives is a completely different word. For example:

  good – better

  little – less

  much – more
- We add *more* or *less* before some adjectives to form their comparative degree. We usually do that with long words. For example:

  beautiful – more beautiful/less beautiful

  expensive – more expensive/less expensive
- We use **than** with comparative adjectives. For example:

  She's taller than Mukul.

  Mumbai is a bigger city than Ujjain.

  Reema is a better football player than her brother.

B. Fill in each blank with the comparative form of the correct adjective from the box.

cheap *fat* *old* *short* *tall* *weak*

1. Iron is .... than gold.
2. The giraffe is .... than a zebra.
3. Riya is three years .... than Surjeet.

4. As a man grows older, he becomes ....

5. The boy did not exercise regularly and as a result he grew ....

6. These stories are .... than the ones my grandmother told me.

LISTENING AND SPEAKING

Listening

A. Regular announcements are made at railway stations, airports, bus terminals, etc. to keep the passengers informed about arrivals and departures. Listen to three announcements made at three different railway stations. Fill in the table accordingly.

Train number	Train name	Starting point	Destination	Platform number	Any other detail
52962			Ratlam		
	New Delhi Shatabdi Express				Expected to depart at 7:20 a.m.
		Bandra Terminus		5	

Speaking

Making suggestions

B. Role-play the following situation with a partner, making appropriate suggestions. After you have finished, change the roles and do the activity again.

Partner : *I am bored. What shall we do?*

You : *Let's* ....

Partner : *No, I don't like playing* ....

You : ....

Partner : *That's a good idea!* ....

You : ....

Partner : *That sounds interesting. Let's start* ....

WRITING

Which character did you like the most in the story? Draw a brief character sketch of the person. Include the qualities of the person in the character sketch and say why you like him/her better than other characters.

8 The Myriad Colours Of Meghalaya

Environment

OBJECTIVES

In this chapter, we will:

- *read about the state Meghalaya.*
- *learn to form adjectives by adding a suffix to nouns.*
- *learn the use of will and can, and some and any.*
- *learn to describe a person.*
- *practise writing a report.*

WARM-UP

Mindfulness Activity
Being mindful of nature around us

A. 1. Go out in the open where you can see the sky. What do you see in the sky? Clouds? Draw the shape of the clouds you have seen in your notebook.

2. Isn't it fun to notice that the clouds resemble other objects? You can name your clouds according to the object.

B. Go to a garden. Walk on the grass or soft mud bare feet. Enjoy the touch of the soft mud on your skin. Write about how you feel.

READING

When you see a map of India, do you look at the seven, small hilly states in the northeast of the country? Now, read about one of those states—Meghalaya.

The entire northeastern region of India is known for its natural beauty and amazing places to visit. There are seven north eastern states in India: Arunachal Pradesh, Assam, Manipur, Mizoram, Nagaland, Tripura and Meghalaya. They are fondly referred to as *The Seven Sisters*. Among all of them, Meghalaya is the most picturesque state.

The word 'Meghalaya' means 'the abode of the clouds' or a place where the clouds live. It is a very apt name because it is often cloudy and is considered to be one of the wettest places in the world. Meghalaya was a part of Assam and became an independent state in the year 1972.

This state is located among the Garo, Khasi and Jentia Hills. It rains almost all year round. Among the Khasi hills of Meghalaya is the beautiful village of Mawsynram, which receives the highest

amazing: striking or brilliant
abode: a home or house

Mountain ridges and clouds in Meghalaya

Earth Speaks

More Wonders in Northeast India

- The Hornbill Festival

  It is a one-of-a-kind festival in Nagaland. It is celebrated from the 1st to the 10th of December. It attracts tourists from all around the world. The festival showcases the rich tribal culture of Nagaland. The traditional crafts, dances, food, art, music, games and sports are displayed.

- Keibul Lamjao National Park

  It is the only floating national park in the world. It is made up of a swamp of a plant called 'phumdis' floating on the surface of the Loktak Lake in Manipur.

rainfall in India. The Garos, the Khasis and the Jentias are the three tribes that live happily in these hills. English is the official language of this state. However, the main tribes have their own languages.

This beautiful state abounds with fantastic forests mountains and valleys. The wet climate supports a variety of flora and fauna. Meghalaya is a storehouse of richly varied and colourful orchids with as many as 325 species, which grow all over the meadows, hill slopes, swamps, and even on the roadside.

The people of the Jentia and the Khasi tribes living deep in the valleys and forests build a unique kind of a bridge—the famous 'living root bridge' of Meghalaya. These bridges are made up of roots of a rubber tree. The roots are entangled and grown in such a way that they touch the opposite bank. The roots are looked after well until they are strong enough to grow and reach the other bank on the opposite side. These bridges are so strong that almost fifty people can walk across it in one go. One of the best living root bridges is a double-decker root bridge located in Cherrapunji. Isn't it amazing? Truly Meghalaya is marvelous!

The unique people of Meghalaya have developed many natural wonders. Another such wonder is the Eri silk. Eri is the most

Living root bridges in Nongriat, Meghalaya

tribe: a group of families
abounds: exists in large numbers
flora and fauna: plants and animals found in a particular area
unique: being the only one of a particular type
entangled: to trap or knot something

respected fabric of the local tribal people of Meghalaya. Maybe that's why hundreds of villages raise these silkworms and have the Eri silk supply chain. When the Eri caterpillar grows to full size, it becomes ready to spin a cocoon around itself. Over a period of time, it develops into a moth, and leaves the cocoon unharmed. In most of the other silk productions, the cocoon is boiled and the silkworms are destroyed in order to procure the silk. However, in case of the Eri silk, the moth emerges out of the cocoon to begin its life. That is why Eri silk is also called the *ahimsa* silk.

The marvels of Meghalaya never stop to amaze. The cleanest and the most **picturesque** of all rivers is also located in Meghalaya! The name of the river is Umngot. The water of the Umngot river is so clear that one can see the bottom of the river and all the marine life in it. People who have enjoyed a boat ride on this river have felt that their boat was floating in the air. Many tourists who come here enjoy fishing, boating, **kayaking** and cliff diving.

Mawlynnong, is a village located at a height of 5,000 feet among the Khasi hills in Meghalaya. This village is called *God's Own Garden* and has enough reasons for that. It was awarded the title The Cleanest Village in Asia. All the villagers take part in the cleanliness **campaign** ensuring that there is no **litter** in the entire village. Children from the village come out early morning on Saturdays to pick up litter as part of the village's compulsory social work program. Someone from each household participates in the daily **ritual**. It is a common sight to see people brooming, collecting garbage, dry leaves and putting them into dustbins made of bamboo! Using dustbins made up of bamboo indicates how conscious the people are about protecting their environment. In fact, it is a community based on the *eco-tourism* **initiative**. It is very interesting to know how the villagers take care of the waste. The dry leaves are buried and converted into manure. There is a strict ban on the use of plastic and other **toxic** materials.

Mawlynnong is **breathtakingly** beautiful. It is covered with lush green forests, waterfalls, small streams, lovely orchid and bougainvillea blossoms that **adorn** the hedges on the pathway. It is especially green and full of flowers after the rains. Every house has

Earth Speaks

- a. Mizoram – is the largest producer of bamboo plant in India.
  b. Tripura – all 184 kings of the Manikya Dynasty ruled this state before Independence.
  c. Assam – The Kaziranga National Park, famous for the one-horned Indian rhinoceros, is also located in Assam. More than 2,200 rhinos are found here.
  d. Arunachal Pradesh – the only place where more than 26 tribes live. It is the largest state among the *Seven Sisters*. This state is home to 500 varieties of orchids.

picturesque: beautiful and attractive
kayaking: using a type of boat 'kayak' to move across water. It uses a double-sided paddle to row.
campaign: a series of activities designed to achieve a goal
litter: rubbish or waste
ritual: regular repeated action
initiative: a plan or the first step
toxic: poisonous
breathtaking: very striking and exciting
adorn: to decorate or enhance

cuisine: regional food preparations
paradise: like heaven
explore: to travel into an unfamiliar region

a natural rainwater basin which gives the houses their unique look. These practices along with the natural beauty of the place makes it look like heaven on earth. A 78-kilometre drive by road from Shillong, the capital city of Meghalaya, will take you to this village.

A visit to Meghalaya cannot be complete without visiting Shillong. It is undoubtedly a beautiful hill station but what makes it unique is the tradition of music here. It is popularly known as the 'rock capital of India'. It has a tradition of rock music that dates as far back as the 1970s. Shillong has given India some of the best musical bands. The Shillong Chamber Choir, the Soulmate and the Aberrant are some of the famous rock bands.

Meghalaya never stops to amaze you, whether it is the food, the variety of cultures, languages, cuisine, the festivals, the clothing, or the dances. It is a tourist paradise and a must visit for those who have yet not explored the beauty of India.

SUMMARY

The lesson talks about the beautiful state of Meghalaya, located in the north-eastern part of India. Its marvels and uniqueness is brought out by its geography, culture and natural resources. It literally means 'abode of clouds'. Meghalaya houses many natural wonders of the world such as the 'living root bridge', the Eri silk, the picturesque village Mawlynnong and the cleanest river Umngot. The Garo, the Khasi and the Jentia tribes reside here. This state is a tourist paradise comprising beautiful valleys, mountains, and forests, offering a wide variety of experiences for all.

COMPREHENSION

A. Choose the correct option.

1. The seven north eastern states of India are called the
   a. Seven Brothers.
   b. Seven Sisters.
   c. Seven States.
2. Meghalaya became an independent state in
   a. 1792.
   b. 1927.
   c. 1972.

3. .... is a village in Meghalaya which receives the highest rainfall in India.
   a. Manipur
   b. Mawsynram
   c. Mizoram

4. Which trees are used to make the famous 'living root bridges' of Meghalaya?
   a. Rubber
   b. Orchid
   c. Bougainvillea

5. Among which hills is the village of Mawlynnong located?
   a. Garo Hills
   b. Khasi Hills
   c. Jentia Hills

B. Answer the questions.

1. Why is the name 'Meghalaya' apt for the state?
2. How do the tribal people make the 'living root bridges'?
3. What is unique about Eri silk?
4. Describe the waters of the Umngot river.
5. How do the villagers take part in the cleanliness campaign in Mawlynnong?
6. What is Shillong known as and why?

Life Skills and Values

Caring for the environment

1. While travelling with your family to a hill station, you see that many tourists litter the place. Do you think it is the correct thing to do? How should we preserve our natural environment?
2. Reducing, recycling and reusing waste are eco-friendly practices. How do you think you can adapt these practices in your school?

VOCABULARY

Suffixes

- A **suffix** is a letter or a group of letters placed at the end of a word to form a new word with a different meaning. For example:

  beauty + ful = beautiful *amaze + ing = amazing*

- Sometimes we can form describing words or adjectives by simply adding the letter 'y' to the end of the root word. For example:

  oil+ y = oily

Fill in the banks with suitable describing words. Form them by adding the suffix- 'y' to the root words in the box.

cloud rain water wind silk hand curl

1. The weather was .... when we reached Meghalaya.
2. The .... day was ideal for kite flying.
3. The scarf was .... and shiny.
4. Gunjan has .... hair.
5. The .... season has set in the hills.
6. A pocket torch can come in .... while you are travelling.
7. The milk shake was .... and not thick.

GRAMMAR

Will and *can*

- Verbs that are used with other verbs to express possibility, intention, or ability are known as **modals** or **modal auxiliary verbs**. Let's look at the usage of two common modals, will and can.

Will

- We use will
  - to talk about the future.

    *The birds **will** eat all the cherries.*

  - to make predictions or simple statements of fact about the future.

    *You **will** become a good cricketer.*

- to state decisions that are made at the time of speaking.

  I will carry the bag for you.
- to talk about what people want to do or are willing to do.

  My sister will water the plants.
- to make promises and offers.

  I will help you with your homework.
- with expressions like *I think, I guess,* and *I hope.*

  I think your brother will like these shoes.

Can

- We use **can**
  - to express ability.

    I can solve this problem easily.
  - to ask for and give permission.

    You can use my pen.

    Can I borrow your eraser, please?

A. Fill in each blank with *can* or *will*.

1. I .... travel to Meghalaya next summer.
2. Mehul .... swim very fast.
3. .... you name one of the tribes of Meghalaya?
4. Feroz .... enjoy a boat ride on the Umngot river.
5. .... you name the place which receives the highest rainfall in India?

Some and *any*

Some

- We use **some**
  - before uncountable nouns to mean *an amount of.*

    Please have some juice.
  - before plural nouns to mean *a number of* or *a few.*

    Please give me some biscuits.

Any

- We use **any**
  - before uncountable nouns and plural nouns in negative statements and questions.

    Did you bring any bread?

    Liza refused to answer any questions.
  - before a singular countable noun when it does not matter which one.

B. Fill in each blank with *some* or *any*.

1. We met .... tourists on our way to Shillong.
2. Do you have .... idea about good hotels in Gangtok?
3. I have .... photographs of the picnic.
4. Suresh did not have .... information about the hill station.
5. She could watch .... of the dances at the festival.

LISTENING AND SPEAKING

Listening

A. Your school is organising activities to celebrate Environment Day. Listen to the announcement and complete the form.

Event	For classes	Topic	Date, time, and venue	Details
Drawing competition				
Pot-painting competition				
Fancy-dress competition				
English poetry recitation competition				

Speaking

Communication Collaboration

B. Work in pairs. Paste pictures of your family vacation in the frame below. Describe the beautiful places you visited. Talk about the weather, the food, the dress and any other special feature about this place.

WRITING

Imagine your school organized a 'Cleanliness Drive' in the neighbourhood recently. Write a brief report on the drive. Include the following points in your report.

- When and where was the **cleanliness drive** held?
- Who participated in this drive?
- What was done by the participants?
- What was the main purpose of the drive?

....

....

....

....

....

....

....

....

....

....

....

....

....

....

....

....

....

....

9 How the Leaves Came Down

Environment

OBJECTIVES

In this chapter, we will:

- *read and understand a poem about leaves falling down trees.*
- *learn synonyms and antonyms.*
- *learn to make a leaf family.*

WARM-UP

Mindfulness Activity

Appreciating nature

Take a leaf walk in your school campus. Collect two different types of leaves. Observe and write the following details about the leaves.

- Colours and shapes of the leaves
- Names of the trees
- Compare the colours of the fallen leaves and the leaves on the tree

Colour: ....
Shape: ....
Name of tree: ....
Comparison: ....

Stick the leaf here

Colour: ....
Shape: ....
Name of tree: ....
Comparison: ....

Stick the leaf here

READING

Do you know why leaves fall in autumn?
Read this poem by Susan Coolidge to find out.

'I'll tell you how the leaves came down,'
The great Tree to his children said:
'You're getting sleepy, Yellow and Brown,
Yes, very sleepy, little Red.
It is quite time to go to bed.'
'Ah!' begged each silly, pouting leaf,
'Let us a little longer stay;
Dear Father Tree, behold our grief!'
'Tis such a very pleasant day,
We do not want to go away.'
So, for just one more merry day
To the great Tree the leaflets clung,
Frolicked and danced, and had their way,
Upon the autumn breezes swung,
Whispering all their sports among—
'Perhaps the great Tree will forget,
And let us stay until the spring,
If we all beg, and coax, and fret.'

begged: asked or requested sincerely
silly: foolish; unimportant
pouting: pushing one's lips forward as an expression of annoyance
behold: to see; look at (old English)
grief: another word for sadness
'tis: contraction of 'it is'
merry: happy
leaflets: (here) young leaves
clung: held on tightly
frolicked: played or moved about in a cheerful and lively way
coax: to persuade someone gradually or gently to do something
fret: (here) to want something by asking for it again and again

But the great Tree did no such thing;

He smiled to hear their whispering.

'Come, children, all to bed,' he cried;

And ere the leaves could urge their prayer,

He shook his head, and far and wide,

Fluttering and rustling everywhere,

Down sped the leaflets through the air.

I saw them; on the ground they lay,

Golden and red, a huddled swarm,

Waiting till one from far away,

White bedclothes heaped upon her arm,

Should come to wrap them safe and warm.

The great bare Tree looked down and smiled.

'Goodnight, dear little leaves,' he said.

And from below each sleepy child replied,

'Goodnight,' and murmured,

'It is so nice to go to bed!'

Literary Device

- In the poem, the tree speaks and so do the leaves. Sometimes, a thing or an idea is represented as a person, especially in poetry. Such a usage is known as **personification**.
- Personification means presenting an animal or a thing as having a human quality.
- The word personification contains the word *person*, and to personify an object means to describe it as if it were a person.
- Instead of saying that the sun is shining, we could say that the sun is smiling down at us.
- Instead of describing a flag as fluttering in the wind, we could say that the flag is dancing in the wind.

ere: before (old English)
urge: to persistently persuade someone to do something
fluttering: moving with a light irregular or trembling motion
rustling: making a soft, muffled sound like that caused by the movement of dry leaves
huddled: crowded together in a small space
swarm: a large number

SUMMARY

Leaves fall during autumn. The poet has described the tree as a father. His children are the leaves. The tree coaxes the leaves to go off to sleep. The leaves which are named after their colour are yellow, brown and red. The leaves beg their father to play for one more day. The leaves have their way. Finally, the next day the tree shakes its branches in the autumn wind. The leaves come rustling down on the ground and wait for the snowy blanket to cover them.

COMPREHENSION

A. Choose the correct option.

1. The leaves did not want to go to sleep as
   a. they loved to sing.
   b. it was a pleasant day.
   c. they wanted to listen to a story.

2. The leaves wanted to stay until
   a. spring.
   b. the monsoon.
   c. the next summer.
3. When all the leaves came down, the Tree was
   a. full.
   b. bare.
   c. heavy.

B. Read these lines from the poem and answer the questions.

1. *You're getting sleepy, Yellow and Brown,*
   Yes, very sleepy, little Red
   It is quite time to go to bed.
   a. Who says that?
   b. Why do you think the speaker addresses the listeners as *Yellow, Brown,* and *Red*?
2. *White bedclothes heaped upon her arm,*
   Should come to wrap them safe and warm.
   a. What do you understand by *white bedclothes* here?
   b. Who will be wrapped safe and warm?

C. Answer the questions.

1. Who tells the story of the falling of leaves in the poem?
2. Who are Yellow, Brown, and little Red in the poem?
3. What do the leaves not want to do?
4. What happens when the great Tree shakes his head?
5. What is personified in the lines, 'White bedclothes heaped upon her arm'?
6. Do you think the poem describes children's nature? Give reasons to support your answer.

Life Skills and Values — **Appreciating nature**

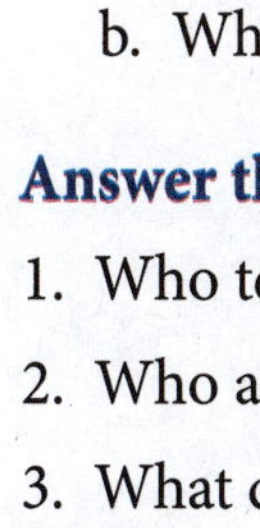

1. Each season has its own importance. Trees look bare when the leaves fall. How do trees look during the spring and the monsoon? Why?
2. We often talk about summer heat or winter cold with a dislike. Why do you think they happen? Do you think nature as a purpose for hot summers and cold winters as well? Explain your thoughts.

VOCABULARY

Synonyms and antonyms

- **Synonyms** are words that have the same or nearly the same meanings. For example: *cold* and *cool*.
- **Antonyms** are words that have opposite meanings. For example: *cold* and *hot*.

A. Write 'S' next to word pairs that are synonyms. Write 'A' next to word pairs that are antonyms.

1. beneath	above	☐
2. feasting	fasting	☐
3. few	many	☐
4. flower	blossom	☐
5. pale	dull	☐
6. silence	quiet	☐
7. small	tiny	☐
8. strong	sturdy	☐
9. tall	short	☐
10. top	bottom	☐

B. Find words in the poem which mean the following.

1. stupid ....
2. to enjoy ....
3. answered ....
4. a young leaf ....

ACTIVITY

Making a leaf family

Go on a leaf-hunting walk. Collect leaves that have fallen down on the ground. Make sure you collect different kinds of leaves—long, round, broad, etc.

Take one leaf and paste it on a thick white sheet of paper. Stick the leaf in a way that it resembles the body of a human being, an animal, or a bird. Draw a face, arms, legs, a tail, etc. outside the leaf to complete the living being. Make a family with the leaves you have collected.

10 The Three Questions

Finding solutions

OBJECTIVES

In this chapter, we will:

- *read a short story about a king looking for the answers to three important questions.*
- *learn proverbs and their meanings.*
- *learn to use should and shouldn't.*
- *learn to use let me and let's/let us.*
- *learn to plan a future event.*
- *practise writing an account of past experiences.*

WARM-UP

Mindfulness Activity

Being mindful of the present moment

A. Now—The Present Moment

The word *present* means the moment in time that is right now. It also means a gift. Think about it: can the present moment be a gift of time? Should we then use it wisely and well? Sit quietly and feel what is going on *right now* using your senses. Then, complete the worksheet.

1. RIGHT NOW, I see ....
2. RIGHT NOW, I hear ....
3. RIGHT NOW, I smell ....
4. RIGHT NOW, I am touching ....
5. RIGHT NOW, I feel ....

B. Be in the Present Moment

Draw a happy experience you had in the past, something that you are looking forward to in the future, and something which is happening *right now*.

Past	Future	Present

READING

A king has three questions, to which he finds no answers from his courtiers. What happens when he visits an old hermit in a forest to search for his answers? Read on to find out.

> **secret:** something that it is known by only a small number of people, and is not told or shown to anyone else

There was once a king who believed that the **secret** to never fail was to know the answer of three questions. These three questions were: when was the right time to begin a task?; who were the people to be with and who were to avoid?; and, what was the most important thing to do?

As a king ought to, he pondered on these questions. After having pondered enough, he declared them to his subjects and announced great rewards to anyone who would answer them correctly.

From far and wide, wise people gathered to the king's court, and tried their best to answer these three questions. But each answered these questions differently, and the king was left perplexed and dissatisfied. And the rewards were given to none.

Finally, the king heard of a hermit who was deemed to be very wise. But the hermit lived alone in a forest and met only the common folk. So, the king gave up his royal robes, dressed simply and went forth to visit this hermit.

When the king came to the hermitage, he found the hermit to be old, frail and busily digging flower beds outside his hut. The king walked to the hermit and said, 'I am the king. And I have come to find the answer to three questions. Tell me, when should be the right time to do something? And who is the right person to be with, over others? Which work is the most important to do?' But the hermit did not reply and continued to dig the earth. The king watched for a while. The aged hermit could only turn over a little earth and wheezed every time he lifted the spade and struck the ground. So, out of humanity, the king offered to dig the flower beds for him.

Fact File

The king in the story sought the help of a hermit. Indian history recounts many such famous hermits who changed the history of India. *Vyasa* was a hermit and a sage who is considered the author of the *Mahabharata*. Another sage and hermit *Patanjali* wrote the *Yoga Sutra*, an important book on yoga.

pondered: thought about something carefully
perplexed: confused and slightly worried
hermit: a monk or a person who lives alone and away from society
deemed: considered to have a particular quality
hermitage: the home of a hermit
frail: weak
wheezed: breathed with difficulty, making a whistling sound
humanity: the quality of being kind and thoughtful

He dug two beds, then paused and asked the hermit the three questions again. The hermit said nothing, but rose and offered to take the spade, saying, 'Now rest awhile, and let me work a bit'. But the king refused and continued to dig.

A few hours passed. When the sun began to sink behind the trees, the king stopped and said, 'I came to you, wise man, for an answer to my questions. If you can give me none, tell me so, and I will return home.'

'Here comes someone running,' said the hermit, 'let us see who it is.'

A bearded man came running out of the woods. He was **wounded** in his stomach. When he reached the hermitage, he fainted. The hermit and the king quickly attended to the stranger's wounds. They managed to stop the bleeding and carried the stranger inside the hermit's hut, so that he could rest and recover in safety.

The sun had set, it was cool and dark. The king was **exhausted** with the events of the day. So, he slept soundly throughout the short summer night, lying in the **threshold** of the hermitage.

The next morning, the stranger spoke to the king and asked for his forgiveness. Surprised, the king said, 'I do not know you, and have nothing to forgive you for'. The stranger then said that he was the king's enemy, who wanted to kill him. But because the king was at the hermitage and not in the royal palace, he got caught by the king's guard and was wounded as he escaped. Now, he had been saved by the king himself and would forever be grateful to him. The king was glad that his enemy made peace with him.

Finally, the king arranged to leave, and he went to the hermit again. The hermit was on his knees, sowing seeds in the flower beds that were dug the day before. The king said, 'For the last time, I pray you to answer my questions, wise man.'

The hermit replied without looking up, 'You have been answered.'

'How answered? What do you mean?' asked the king.

'Do you not see'. replied the hermit. 'If you had not pitied my weakness yesterday, and had not dug those beds for me, but had

wounded: injured or hurt
exhausted: tired
threshold: the floor at the doorway

gone your way, that man would have attacked you. So, the most important time was when you were digging the beds; and I was the most important man; and to do me good was your most important business.

Afterwards when that man ran to us, the most important time was when you were attending to him, for if you had not bound up his wounds, he would have died without having made peace with you. So, he was the most important man, and what you did for him was your most important business.

Remember then: there is only one time that is important—now! It is the most important time because it is the only time when we have any power. The most important person is one with whom you are, for no one knows whether he or she will ever have dealings with anyone else; and the most important work is, to do good to the person you are with, because for that purpose alone humans have been sent into this life!'

Fact File

The story *The Three Questions* is a **parable** which means that it is a story with a moral value. Indian literature is full of such stories. One such example is the *Hitopadesha*, a collection of fables and parables. These stories were written in the Sanskrit language. They impart values and knowledge in a simple and effective manner.

SUMMARY

A king wishes to seek answers to his three questions: when is the right time to begin something; who is the right person to be with; and, what is the most important thing for him to do? When his courtiers fail to answer them correctly, he approaches a wise hermit. Upon reaching the hermitage, the king finds the hermit struggling to dig a flower bed. The king asks his questions but the hermit continues his work. The king helps the hermit till late in the evening. Suddenly, a wounded man comes running to the hermitage. The king and the hermit nurse his wounds and save his life. The man thanks the king and reveals that he was the king's enemy. He was wounded by the king's soldiers while he was waiting to kill the king. He asks forgiveness and makes peace with the king. Before going away, the king again requests the hermit to answer his questions. The hermit replies that his questions were answered: the right time is now, the right person to be with is the one he is with currently, and the most important thing to do is to do good to the person he is with.

COMPREHENSION

A. Choose the correct option.

1. The King believed that
   a. he would never fail.
   b. the secret to never fail was to know the answers to three questions.
   c. the secret to succeed was to know the answers to all questions.
2. The king was perplexed and dissatisfied because
   a. all the wise men gave different answers to his questions.
   b. all the wise men gave the same answers to his questions.
   c. all the wise men gave answers that made no sense.
3. The hermit in the forest was
   a. young and fat.
   b. old and grumpy.
   c. old and frail.
4. The bearded man from the forest was
   a. wounded in the leg.
   b. wounded in the stomach.
   c. wounded in the head.

5. The wounded man was
   a. the king's enemy.
   b. a hunter who was hurt.
   c. a thief who was wounded .

B. Complete the sentences.

1. The King announced great rewards to

2. The King gave up his royal robes and dressed simply because

3. The hermit was helped by the king in digging because

4. The bearded stranger asked for the king's forgiveness because

C. Answer the questions.

1. The answers to which three questions did the king believe were the secret to never failing?
2. Why did the king go to the hermit?
3. What was the hermit doing when the king met him?
4. Who was the bearded stranger?
5. What were the hermit's answers to each of the three questions?

Life Skills and Values

Finding solutions

1. Actions speak louder than words. What all did the king do to find a solution for his situation?
   Think of a situation that you are finding difficult to deal with. What can you do to move towards a solution for it?
2. The hermit explains to the king that the present moment is the most important time. How can you adopt this advice in your everyday life?

VOCABULARY

Proverbs

- **Proverbs** are sentences that state a general truth or piece of advice. For example, the proverb *an apple a day keeps the doctor away* suggests eating fruits daily is good for health.
- Here are some more examples of proverbs and their meanings.

  Honesty is the best policy. → One should always speak the truth.

  Laughter is the best medicine. → Trying to be happy is a good way to stop worrying.

A. Match each proverb with its meaning. You can use a dictionary or the Internet for help.

Proverb	Meaning
1. Actions speak louder than words.	a. A good beginning almost always leads to success.
2. A journey of a thousand miles begins with a single step.	b. Being clean is a sign of spiritual purity or goodness.
3. Birds of a feather flock together.	c. However big a task may be, the process of achieving it always begins with a small action.
4. Cleanliness is next to godliness.	d. People like the company of those people who are like them.
5. Well begun is half done.	e. What a person does is more important than what he or she says.

GRAMMAR

Should and *shouldn't*

- *Should* and *shouldn't* are **modals** or **auxiliary verbs**, which are used with other verbs to express necessity.
- We use *should* and *shouldn't* to give advice or to talk about what is right or wrong. For example:

  You should take care of your dog.

  We shouldn't fight with our classmates.

A. Fill in each blank with *should* or *shouldn't*.

1. We .... harm plants.
2. Rakesh, you .... drown the cherry plant.
3. You .... take an umbrella, as it might rain.
4. We .... grow more trees to protect the environment.
5. Rakesh .... be upset, as the cherry tree is tough. It will grow again.

Making offers

Let me + verb

- We use **let me** + verb to make an offer. For example:

  Let me help you with your homework.

  Here, the person speaking is offering to help with the listener's homework.

Let us

- We use **let us** or **let's** to make a suggestion. For example:

  Let's visit the science fair.

  Here the speaker is suggesting that they should visit the science fair.

B. Read the sentences. Write O for an offer and S for a suggestion.

1. Let's watch a film this evening. ☐
2. Let's enjoy the holidays at my place. ☐
3. Let me carry your luggage to the taxi. ☐
4. Let us help the old couple cross the road. ☐
5. The sun is too hot today; let me water the plants. ☐
6. Mother is unwell; let me go and buy vegetables today. ☐

LISTENING AND SPEAKING

Listening

A. Listen to a boy telling you about himself and fill in the details about him in the form below.

Form for Joining Dance Classes

Name : ....

Age : ....

Address : ....

City : ....

State : ....

Phone number : ....

Type of dance to be learnt : ....

....

Preferred time slot : ....

....

Speaking

Communication Collaboration

B. Imagine you are planning a surprise birthday party for your brother or sister. Work in pairs and share your plans with your partner. Let your partner give his/her suggestions to you. You can begin like this:

It will be great fun. Let us ...

WRITING

Creative Thinking

Travelogue writing

- A travelogue is a film, book, or an illustrated account about the places visited by a traveller or his/her experiences during the journey.
- Travelogues can be written during the period of the journey or after that.
- When you write a travelogue, you should recollect all that happened during the travel, and should include the following information:

  1. Where did you go?
  2. When did you go there?

3. Who did you go with?
4. How long did you stay there?
5. What did you do during the vacation?
6. Would you like to go there again? Why/Why not?

Have you ever gone on a vacation? Write a short travelogue about your experience using the hints from above. Paste photographs or draw pictures of your vacation.

PROJECT 2

Creative Thinking

TRAVELOGUE

A family holiday is always fun. No matter what your destination is, you will definitely want to share the details with your friends. Writing your own travelogue is a nice way to do so.
Here are some steps to be followed while writing one:

1. Present all interesting events that have happened in a chronological order.
2. You can divide your travelogue into different sections:
    - Transport: how did you travel?
    - Description: which place did you visit?
    - Climate: what was the weather like? Cold? Warm?
    - Accommodation: the hotels you stayed in or the restaurants you visited.
3. The local cuisine of a place must always be tried while on a vacation. Do not forget to include a recipe of the local delicacy that you enjoyed.
4. Add pictures which you clicked during your travel.
5. How was this place different from your home town? Mention the differences and some of the interesting observations you made about the people living there.
6. You can make a PowerPoint presentation and show it to your entire class.

11 The Praying Hands

Art and creativity

OBJECTIVES

In this chapter, we will:

- *read a story of brotherly love and sacrifice.*
- *learn portmanteau words.*
- *learn to add the suffixes -ed and -ing to words ending in l.*
- *learn about subject-verb agreement.*
- *learn to form and use simple past and past continuous tenses.*
- *listen to a description of Rani Lakshmibai's life and put sentences in order.*
- *learn to request action for a noble cause.*
- *learn to pronounce words with the short o sound.*
- *practise writing a biography.*

WARM-UP

21st Century Skills — Critical Thinking

A. Read the clues and solve the crossword puzzle on art.

Across

1. paints or colours that we mix with water and use for painting pictures
4. a picture that has been painted

Down

2. the art of quickly drawing pictures that don't have many details
3. the art of making a picture by sticking pieces of coloured paper, cloth, or photographs onto a surface

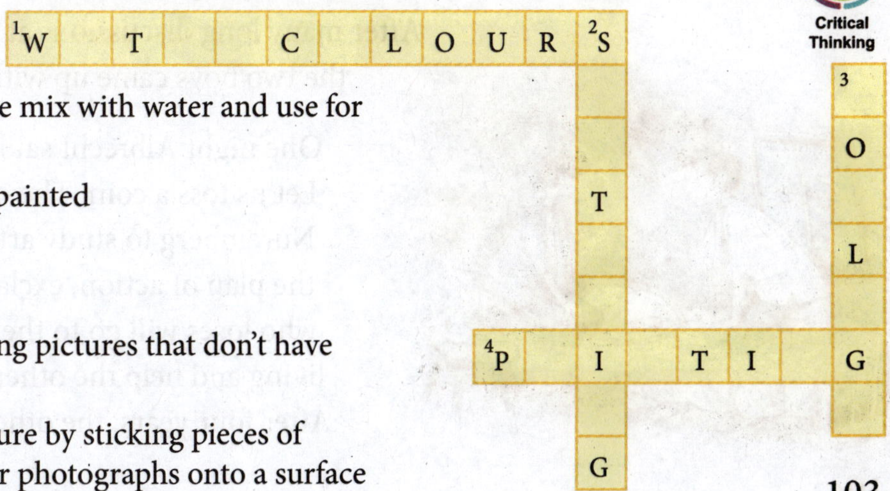

Mindfulness Activity

Appreciating our body parts

B. THE PRAYING HANDS

Take a sheet of paper. Put your palm on it and trace your hand with a pencil on the paper. Write down three things that you can do with your hands. Colour the traced hand carefully without spilling over the lines.

Three things that I can do with my hands:

1. ....

2. ....

3. ....

READING

goldsmith: a person who makes articles such as jewellery
household: a house and its occupants regarded as a unit
pursue: to follow or chase (someone or something)
enrol: to officially register to join or become a member of an institution or a student on a course
financial: relating to money
discussions: conversations about a specific topic
crowded: full of people, leaving little or no room for movement; packed
mines: places where deep holes or tunnels are dug under the ground to extract coal, diamonds, gold, or other minerals

Read this real story about the renowned painting 'The Praying Hands' by the famous painter Albrecht Dürer (Ayl-brekt Dyurer).

In the fifteenth century, a goldsmith named Albrecht Dürer (the elder), lived in a small village near Nuremberg, a German town. He lived with his wife and eighteen children. As the father and the head of the household, and to feed his huge family, he worked almost eighteen hours a day.

Despite their seemingly hopeless condition, two of Albrecht Dürer's children had a dream. They were Albert and Albrecht, the latter named after his father. Both brothers wanted to pursue their dream of becoming artists. They wanted to enrol themselves in the school of art at Nuremberg, but they knew it would be impossible knowing their father's financial condition.

After many long discussions at night in their crowded bed, the two boys came up with a plan.

One night Albrecht said, 'Albert! I have an idea. Let us toss a coin. The one who wins will go to Nuremberg to study art.' Albert, who understood the plan of action, exclaimed at once, 'Yes! The one who loses will go to the nearby mines and earn a living and help the other to complete his studies. After four years, the other brother can study.'

The two brothers were very excited. Albert tossed the coin on a Sunday morning after church. Albrecht won the toss and went off to Nuremberg. Albert went down into the dangerous mines and, for the next four years, earned money for his brother's studies. Very soon, Albrecht's work became very popular and he started earning money. People began to admire his paintings, and he became a famous artist.

When the young artist returned to his village, the Dürer family held a festive dinner on their lawn to celebrate Albrecht's homecoming. After a long and memorable meal, Albrecht rose from his chair and announced, 'I owe this popularity to my dearest brother, whose help and support have helped me achieve success and fulfil my dream of becoming an artist.' His closing words were, 'And now, Albert, blessed brother of mine, now it is your turn. Now you can go to Nuremberg to pursue your dream, and I will take care of you.'

All heads turned in eager expectation to the far end of the table where Albert sat with tears streaming down his pale face. He shook his lowered head from side to side while he sobbed and repeated, over and over, 'No… no… no.'

Finally, Albert rose and wiped the tears off his cheeks. He glanced down the long table at the faces he loved. Then, holding his hands close to his right cheek, he said softly, 'No, brother. I cannot go to Nuremberg. It is too late for me. Look what four years in the mines have done to my hands! The bones in every finger have been smashed at least once, and lately I have been suffering from severe pain in my right hand that I cannot even hold a glass, much less make delicate lines on a paper or canvas with a pen or a brush. No brother, it is too late for me.'

One day, to pay homage to Albert for all that he had sacrificed, Albrecht Dürer drew his brother's abused hands with palms together and thin fingers stretched skyward. He called his powerful drawing simply *Hands* but the entire world almost immediately opened their hearts to his great masterpiece and renamed his tribute of love *The Praying Hands*.

Looking Back

- A museum is a building where things of artistic, cultural, historic, and scientific interest are kept and shown to the public.
- The Albertina is a museum situated in Vienna, Austria.
- It houses one of the largest and most important print collections in the world, with approximately 65,000 drawings and nearly one million old master prints.

festive: relating to a festival; cheerful and celebratory
homecoming: an occasion of returning home
memorable: worth remembering or easily remembered, especially because of being special or unusual
popularity: the state of being liked by many people
eager: strongly wanting to do or have something; keen
streaming: moving in a continuous flow
glanced: took a brief or hurried look
smashed: violently or badly broken or shattered
severe: very great; intense
canvas: a strong heavy cloth on which an artist does a painting
homage: special honour or respect shown publicly
abused: (here) mistreated
masterpiece: an excellent painting, novel, film, or other work of art that has been made with great skill
tribute: something said or done to show admiration and respect for someone

masterful: showing great skill
portraits: paintings, drawings, or photographs of someone, often of only their head and shoulders
silver-point: an old style of drawing by dragging a pointed silver wire across a surface
charcoals: paintings made using a black substance made by burning wood slowly in an oven with little air
woodcuts: prints made from patterns cut in pieces of wood
copper: a soft reddish-brown metal used for making electric wires, coins, etc.
engravings: images made by cutting designs on pieces of metal and then printing the designs on paper

More than 450 years have passed, but till this day, hundreds of **masterful portraits**, pen and **silver-point** sketches, watercolours, **charcoals**, **woodcuts**, and **copper engravings** by Albrecht Dürer hang in every great museum in the world.

Self-portrait of Albrecht Dürer

The Praying Hands

Remember the next time you see a copy of that touching creation, take a second look. Let it be your reminder, if you still need one, that no one ever makes it alone!

SUMMARY

Albrecht Durer, a goldsmith lived in a small German town of Nuremberg. He lived there with his wife and eighteen children. They were poor. Two of his sons Albrecht and Albert dreamt of becoming artists. The brothers think of a plan. They would toss a coin; the winner would study art and the other brother would work in the mines to support his education. Albrecht won the toss and went to the art school whereas Albert stayed on to work in the mines. After four years Albrecht returns as a famous artist. He asks his brother to join the art school. Albert reveals that it was too late as his hands were damaged due to the hardships faced while working in the mines. Albrecht draws his brother's abused hands as a tribute to his sacrifice.

COMPREHENSION

A. Choose the correct option.

1. Where did Albrecht Dürer (the elder) live?
   a. He lived in France.
   b. He lived in England.
   c. He lived in Germany.
2. What was the dream of the two Dürer brothers?
   a. They both wanted to become artists.
   b. They both wanted to become miners.
   c. They both wanted to become goldsmiths.
3. How did the Dürer family celebrate Albrecht's homecoming?
   a. The family held a festive lunch.
   b. The family held a festive dinner.
   c. The family offered prayers at church.
4. What had happened to Albert's hands?
   a. They were just dirty.
   b. They were very hard.
   c. They were injured and pained severely.
5. What was the name given by Albrecht to his painting which was a tribute to his brother Albert?
   a. *Hands*
   b. *The Noble Hands*
   c. *The Praying Hands*

B. Number the events from 1 to 5 in the order they occur in the story.

- [ ] Albert worked in the mines to support his brother's education.
- [ ] When it was Albert's turn, his hands were too injured to hold a brush.
- [ ] The two brothers tossed a coin to decide who would go to the school of art.
- [ ] Albrecht Dürer won the toss and went to Nuremberg to study at the school of art.
- [ ] People began to recognise the talent of Albrecht Dürer and he became famous.

C. Answer these questions.

1. How many children did Albrecht Dürer (the elder) have?
2. What dream did Albrecht and Albert have?
3. To whom did Albrecht give the credit for his success and popularity?
4. Where is *The Praying Hands* kept now?
5. Why do you think Albrecht Dürer painted the hands of his brother?

Life Skills and Values — **Gratitude**

1. If you were in place of Albrecht, what would you do for your brother?
2. Think of the people who have helped you in any way. How would you express your gratitude to those people?

VOCABULARY

Portmanteau words

- **Portmanteau words** blend the spelling and sounds of two words. For example:

  Brunch is formed by combining parts of two words: *breakfast* and *lunch.*
- Portmanteau words also blend the meanings of two words.

Here are some word pairs. Write the portmanteau word that is formed by combining parts of the words in each pair.

1. helicopter + airport = ...
2. high + technology = ...
3. international + network = ...
4. telephone + communication = ...
5. television + broadcast = ...

DICTIONARY SKILLS

Spelling rule

If a verb ends in *l* and has a single vowel, we need to double the *l* while adding the suffix *-ed* or *-ing* to the verb. For example:

travel: travelled, travelling

Add the given suffix to the end of each word. You can consult a dictionary to check whether you need to double the *l*.

1. cancel + ed = ...
2. control +ed = ...
3. equal + ing = ...
4. label + ing = ...
5. model + ing = ...

GRAMMAR

Subject-verb agreement

- The **verb** in a sentence must agree with the **subject**, in number.

  If the subject is singular, the verb must also be singular.

  If the subject is plural, the verb must be plural too.
- In the simple present tense, plurals of nouns and verbs are formed in opposite ways. We add an *-s* to the end of most singular nouns to make them plural while adding an *-s* to the end of a verb makes it singular. For example:

  The bird sits on the branch. (bird= singular noun; sits = singular verb)

  The birds sit on the branch. (birds = plural noun; sit = plural verb)
- If the subject consists of two nouns or pronouns, the verb should be plural. For example:

  Ravi and Lina are friends.

  Some goats and cows were grazing grass by the river.

A. Fill in each blank with the correct verb form.

1. Where .... (*does/do*) they live?
2. Parul and Manav .... (*like/likes*) grapes.
3. The hills .... (*are/is*) covered with trees.
4. Children .... (*loves/love*) to eat cherries.
5. He .... (*walks/walk*) to school every day.
6. Rinzen .... (*live/lives*) with his grandfather.
7. The gardener .... (*water/waters*) the garden daily.
8. He and his brother .... (*play/plays*) tennis every evening.

Simple past tense

- The **simple past tense** is used to talk about something that happened in the past.
- This tense uses the **past tense** of the verb, such as *became*, *came*, *cleaned*, *sang*, and *worked*.

  Albrecht Dürer became a famous artist.

  Albert Dürer worked in a mine.

B. Fill in each blank using the simple past tense of a suitable verb.

attend   bark   cook   visit   wash   win

1. Who .... your clothes?
2. The dog .... at the visitors.
3. Albrecht .... an art school.

4. I .... my grandparents yesterday.
5. My brother .... dinner for all of us last evening.
6. India .... the 2011 Cricket World Cup.

Past continuous tense

- The **past continuous tense** is used to talk about an action that was going on at some point in time in the past.
- To form the past continuous tense, we use **was/were + verb+ing**. For example:

  I was sleeping at that time.

  The baby was crying.

  The children were playing hockey.

- We use *was* with singular subjects.
- We use *were* with plural subjects.

C. Fill in each blank using the past continuous tense (*was/were* + verb+*ing*) of the verb given in brackets.

1. I .... (*read*) a story.
2. She .... (*go*) to school.
3. The students .... (*make*) a noise.
4. Maliha and her cousins .... (*dance*) in the room.
5. Some children .... (*swim*) in the pond.
6. Ramandeep .... (*play*) on the swing in the park.
7. She .... (*draw*) pictures and colouring them.
8. Bees .... (*collect*) nectar from the flowers in the garden.

LISTENING AND SPEAKING

Listening

A. Listen to a short description of the life of Rani Lakshmibai and number the following sentences in sequence.

- In March 1854, the British ordered Lakshmibai to leave the palace and the fort. ☐
- Rani Lakshmibai was born in Varanasi to a Marathi family. ☐
- The Maharaja died in November 1853. ☐
- She was married to the Maharaja of Jhansi, Raja Gangadhar Rao Newalkar, in May 1842 and became the queen of Jhansi. ☐

- After her marriage, she began to be called Lakshmibai. ☐
- Lakshmibai did not accept the decision of the British and fought against the British army very bravely. ☐
- She died in 1858. ☐
- She was named Manikarnika by her parents. ☐
- She inspired a lot of people to fight for India's independence. ☐
- She was educated at home and learnt shooting, horsemanship, and fencing. ☐

Speaking

21st Century Skills: Communication, Collaboration

B. Work in pairs. Imagine you want to help a poor child buy books. Take turns to request your partner to donate some money for that cause.

Pronunciation

What do the words *rock* and *hot* have in common?

They both have the short *o* sound.

C. Practise saying these words. In each set, circle the word that does not have the short *o* sound.

1. hot	good	pot	shot
2. not	got	goat	odd
3. lop	mom	shoot	off
4. loss	mop	rob	gate
5. lot	tape	sob	top

WRITING

Writing a biography

- A biography is someone's life story written by someone else.
- Here are the steps to follow when writing a biography:
  - Choose whom to write the biography about.
  - The account must be written in chronological order, like what happened first, in time—birth, childhood, education, etc.
  - Write about the main events in his or her life. Write about the achievements and the various stages of the person's life.

Write a short biography of a family member.

12 The Potter

Art and creativity

OBJECTIVES

In this chapter, we will:

- *read and understand a poem about the potter's earthen pots.*
- *learn antonyms.*
- *learn similes.*
- *make a chart on materials used to make pots.*

WARM-UP

Mindfulness Activity

Appreciating handicrafts

A. People use earthen pots and refrigerators to cool water in summer. Can you think of four differences between an earthen pot and a refrigerator?

1. ....
2. ....
3. ....
4. ....

B. Which do you think is more environment-friendly—an earthen pot or a refrigerator? Give reasons for your answer. Is it possible to use an earthen pot in the same way as one uses a refrigerator? Which kind of items that you keep in a refrigerator can be kept in the same way (cool, unspoilt, fresh for long, etc) in an earthen pot?

C. Get mud/clay/soil from your garden or a park or from a nursery nearby. Add a small amount of water and knead them into shape. Think of how the wet feels. You can make small pots, mud balls or toys. Let them dry. Think of how dried mud feels. Decorate what you have made with oil pastel paint.

READING

Have you seen potters make earthen pots? Read the poem by Chitra Padmanabhan to see how their earthen pots help us beat the heat in extremely hot summers.

scorching: very hot
shivers: shaking slightly and uncontrollably because of being cold, frightened, or excited
stoutest: strongest and thickest
lifeline: a thing which someone or something depends on or which provides a means of escape from a difficult situation
piled: placed one on top of the other
tarpaulin: a strong waterproof cloth, originally of canvas
soothe: to gently calm a person or their feelings
slender: thin or narrow
curious: eager to know or learn something
gazelle: a small antelope that has curved horns and a fawn-coloured coat with white underparts, found in Africa and Asia
tucked: put in a secure manner
scowls: frowns in an angry or bad-tempered way
crosser: angrier; more annoyed

The summer sun smiles a scorching smile
The smile sends shivers
Through the stoutest hearts;
A summer smile is reason to sweat
But the potter's back with his cool lifeline!

Earthen pots of every size
Are piled under a tarpaulin sky
Waiting to find new homes
And soothe thirsty throats!

Their water has a magical taste –
The sweet smell of wet earth
Or soil that comes alive after
The first seasonal shower!

Some pots are small, like a baby's song
Some are round—a perfect 'O'
Some are tall with slender necks
Like a curious gazelle looking ahead!

They wait patiently awaiting their turn
To be tucked under a grateful arm
Knowing they give their best
The more the sun scowls, the crosser it gets!

SUMMARY

Chitra Padmanabhan's poem 'The Potter' describes how earthen pots help to quench our thirst in summer. The potter makes the earthen pots himself. These have been called 'lifeline' as they provide cool water to soothe our throats. The water from the earthen pots tastes magical with the sweet smell of the earth. He makes them of all shapes and sizes. The pots are ready to be sold.

COMPREHENSION

A. Choose the correct option.

1. The summer sun is described as
   a. red.
   b. cool.
   c. scorching.
2. The potter has brought earthen pots of
   a. every size.
   b. small size.
   c. large size.
3. The water in the earthen pot has a
   a. sour taste.
   b. salty taste.
   c. magical taste.
4. The pots are waiting
   a. cozily.
   b. patiently.
   c. impatiently.

B. Read these lines from the poem and answer the questions.

1. *A summer smile is reason to sweat*
   But the potter's back with his cool lifeline!
   a. When do we sweat the most?
   b. What does the poet refer to as the 'lifeline'? Why does she say so?
2. *Some pots are small, like a baby's song*
   Some are round—a perfect 'O'
   Some are tall with slender necks
   Like a curious gazelle looking ahead!
   a. What shape do the round pots resemble?
   b. What are the pots with slender necks compared to?

C. Answer these questions.

1. What kind of smile does the summer sun smile?
2. Under what do the earthen pots want to be tucked?

Life Skills and Values — Traditional arts

1. Have you ever used any earthenware made by potters? How do we help them when we use earthen pots and other vessels?
2. Do you think pottery could be taken up as a hobby? Explain your thoughts.
3. What are some of the traditional art forms of the state you belong to? Would you like to learn it as a hobby? Share your thoughts.

VOCABULARY

Antonyms

As we learnt before, **antonyms** are words that have opposite meanings. For example, *dry* and *wet* are antonyms.

A. Find words in the poem which are antonyms of the following words.

1. dead ....
2. worst ....
3. hot ....
4. thick ....

Simile

- A **simile** is a comparison of one thing with another thing of a completely different kind.
- It is used to make a description more emphatic or vivid.
- In the line *some pots are small like a baby's song*, the small pots are compared to the song of a baby.
- While comparing two things in a simile, we use the words *like* or *as*. For example:

as cold as ice *as deep as the ocean* *soft like butter*

B. Match the parts of sentences to complete the similes.

Column A	Column B
1. She is tall like	a. the sky.
2. She is as fast as	b. as snow.
3. He is as slow as	c. a giraffe.
4. The soldier was	d. a tortoise.
5. My shirt is as white	e. a cheetah.
6. The ceiling looks blue like	f. as brave as a lion.

ACTIVITY

Communication Collaboration

Work in groups of four. Use the school library or the Internet to find out about the different materials used to make pots. Write the information collected on a chart paper and illustrate it with drawings or pictures. Display the chart in the class.

13 Liza and the Lost Letter

Play

Determination

OBJECTIVES

In this chapter, we will:

- *read a play about how greed can cause trouble.*
- *learn British and American spellings of words.*
- *learn about genders expressed by words.*
- *learn to identify types of sentences.*
- *listen to two passages and summarise them briefly.*
- *learn to give directions.*
- *practise writing a review of the play.*

WARM-UP

Mindfulness Activity

Knowing that greed leads to trouble

Have you read the story of the greedy dog? Look at the two pictures and describe what you see.

....

....

....

....

....

....

....

....

....

....

READING

Can being greedy cause trouble for one? Read this play by American author Bruce Lansky to find out.

Looking Back

- A king or queen who rules a kingdom is called a monarch and the system of a king or queen's rule is called monarchy.
- Before India got independence in 1947, it had been under the British monarchy for a long time.
- The power to rule India was transferred to Britain by the East India Company in 1858.
- Queen Victoria was the first British Empress of India.

Characters

• Narrator	• Liza Higgins
• Princess Margaret	• Gatekeeper
• Guard	• Appointments Secretary

Narrator: Every Sunday morning at nine o'clock, the **royal** family rides past Liza Higgins' house, and Liza is always waiting on the **sidewalk** in front of her house, waving a little flag—a one-girl welcoming committee.

One Sunday morning in June, as the royal carriage rolled towards her, Liza noticed that Princess Margaret was reading a letter. Suddenly, the letter flew out of the princess's hand into the air. The carriage **jerked** to a stop. The guards **dismounted** and began searching the street. She noticed how **anxious** the princess looked. But the queen seemed **impatient**. She spoke to the driver, and just as suddenly as the **procession** had stopped, the carriage **resumed** moving down the street.

royal: belonging to a king, a queen, or a member of their family
sidewalk: American word for pavement
jerked: made a quick, sharp, or sudden movement
dismounted: got off a vehicle, a horse, or anything that one is riding
anxious: feeling worried or nervous
impatient: annoyed or irritated because you do not want to wait for someone or something
procession: a group of people or vehicle moving together in a line, often as part of a ceremony
resumed: started doing something again after a break

Liza waited until the carriage and guards were out of sight. She walked up the alley where she had seen the letter blow. There, behind a trash barrel was a handwritten letter on fine stationery imprinted with the seal of the king of France. Liza folded the letter carefully and put it in her pocket.

Liza didn't tell a soul about what she had found and decided to walk briskly towards the palace. The gate to the palace was guarded by a gatekeeper who was wearing a tall, bushy, black hat and standing still as a statue.

Liza: Excuse me, I must see Princess Margaret.

Gatekeeper: May I see your pass?

Liza: I don't have a pass.

Gatekeeper: I'm sorry. No one can get through the gate without a pass.

Liza: But you don't understand. I've found something that belongs to the princess. I'm sure she'll want it back.

Gatekeeper: And, no doubt, you will want a reward for your service.

Liza: No. I just want to return to the princess what is hers.

Gatekeeper: In that case, you'll have to have a pass.

Liza: But how will I ever get a pass?

Gatekeeper: I'll be happy to arrange it—for just half of the reward.

Liza: Are you serious?

Narrator: Without even looking at Liza, the gatekeeper simply said...

Gatekeeper: Good day.

Narrator: Liza didn't move. She was angered by the gatekeeper's greed, but the thought of a reward hadn't even occurred to her. So, she reconsidered and said...

Liza: Perhaps I will give you half of the reward.

alley: a narrow passageway between or behind buildings
trash: American word for garbage or waste material
barrel: a wooden container with rounded sides and flat ends
imprinted: stamped on the surface with a mark or outline
briskly: quickly
reconsidered: thought about something again

Narrator: For the first time, the gatekeeper smiled. He took a piece of paper out of his pocket and signed it.

Gatekeeper: Here.

Narrator: Saying that, he opened the gate for Liza and let her in. Another guard escorted Liza to the foyer, where the appointments secretary, who was seated at an ornate wooden desk, was idly turning the pages of a huge appointment book.

Secretary: Who is this urchin?

Guard: Just another beggar looking for a royal reward. She claims she is returning something to the princess.

Secretary: I'm sorry, but Her Majesty's calendar is completely full, for weeks. But, if you'll just give whatever it is to me, I'll see that it is returned to the princess.

Narrator: Liza shook her head.

Liza: You don't understand; this is a personal matter. I must return it to the princess myself.

Secretary: In that case, come back in September and I'll see what I can do. Good day!

Narrator: Liza didn't move. She stared into the eyes of the appointments secretary, so he would know she was serious.

Liza: Why don't you ask Princess Margaret if she's lost something. I think you'll find that she will want to see me immediately.

Secretary: I'll see. If it's that important, then perhaps I can accommodate you. But you'll have to compensate me for my efforts on your behalf. It will cost you half of your reward.

Liza: Agreed.

Secretary: The princess will see you. Remember, I get half of the reward.

Liza: I have an excellent memory.

Narrator: The secretary ushered Liza into Princess Margaret's chamber. As they entered, the princess was pacing the floor. On her face was the same worried expression. He left, closing the polished mahogany door behind him.

escorted: went with another to protect or guide them
appointments secretary: a person who works under another person and arranges his/her meetings
ornate: richly decorated with patterns and designs
urchin: a young child who is poorly or raggedly dressed
Her Majesty: a title given to a queen
immediately: at once; without delay
accommodate: (here) to do a favour; adapt or adjust
compensate: to pay someone for work performed

Princess Margaret: And who might you be?

Liza: Liza Higgins, Your Majesty.

Princess Margaret: I am curious to know, what have you found?

Liza: A letter, Your Majesty. I believe you lost it on the way to church this morning.

Narrator: Liza retrieved the letter from her jacket pocket as the princess approached her.

Princess Margaret: Thank God!

Princess Margaret: Have you read it?

Liza: No.

Narrator: The princess peered into Liza's eyes to see if she was telling the truth.

Liza: I can't understand a word of French.

Narrator: The princess smiled.

Princess Margaret: Have you shown anyone?

Liza: Not a soul, Your Majesty.

Narrator: The princess breathed a sigh of relief.

Princess Margaret: Thank you, Liza. This letter means a great deal to me. Is there anything I can do for you? Name your reward.

retrieved: brought out something from somewhere

Liza: I did not return your letter for a reward. I was just doing what I would have liked someone to do for me. But since you are so kind to offer a reward, I cannot refuse. However, I wonder if you would summon the palace gatekeeper and your appointments secretary. They both helped me to gain an audience with you. I think they will be happy to know that you have granted me a reward.

Princess Margaret: Certainly. *(calling out)* Guard!

Narrator: Instantly, the door opened and a guard appeared.

Princess Margaret: Liza, you have done a great service to me by returning a prized possession. How can I reward you? Your wish is my command.

Narrator: The gatekeeper and the secretary smiled with anticipation.

Liza: Thank you for your generosity, Your Majesty. If you will grant my wish, I humbly request a sentence of two weeks in jail.

Narrator: The faces of the gatekeeper and the secretary turned white. Their jaws dropped open. The princess frowned.

Princess Margaret: I don't understand…

Liza: You see, although I did not seek a reward, the royal gatekeeper, as well as your appointments secretary, made me promise to give him half of my reward in return for letting me in through the palace gate even though I told them both I was here to return something you had lost. I hope that you will grant my request.

Princess Margaret: I cannot refuse your request. *(speaking to guards)* Guards, take the prisoners away. *(turning to Liza)* Young lady, you have done two great services: one to me personally and one to the royal family. I would like to give you another reward.

Narrator: As the princess took a close look at Liza, she said…

Princess Margaret: You look vaguely familiar. Are you the girl who waves to me every Sunday morning as we drive to church?

Liza: Yes, Your Majesty. I wait for you every Sunday. Once you even waved to me.

summon: to order someone to come
anticipation: looking forward to
vaguely: slightly

Princess Margaret: Well, next Sunday, instead of watching me drive by, how would you like to join me for a ride in the royal carriage dressed in a brand-new gown?

Liza: I'd love to!

SUMMARY

Liza Higgins loved to wave at the royal carriage that would pass her house every Sunday morning on their way to the church. One day, she sees Princess Margaret reading a letter. The letter flies off her hands. The guards are unable to find it and they leave without the letter. Liza finds the letter and decides to return it. However, she is not allowed to meet the royal princess until she agrees to pay the guard and the appointments secretary half of her reward which she would receive from the princess. The princess is grateful to Liza and grants her a reward for returning a very important letter. Liza asks for two weeks of imprisonment as her reward. This is gladly divided among the palace gatekeeper and the appointments secretary. Liza's actual reward is a ride in the royal carriage with Princess Margaret.

COMPREHENSION

A. Choose the correct option.

1. The royal family rode past Liza on its way to church
   a. every Sunday morning.
   b. every Monday morning.
   c. every Tuesday morning.
2. The gatekeeper was wearing
   a. a blue hat.
   b. a black hat
   c. a white hat.
3. The appointments secretary asked Liza
   a. to come back after a week.
   b. to come back the next day.
   c. to come back in the month of September.
4. Liza asked the princess
   a. for a gold necklace as her reward.
   b. for two bags of gold coins as her reward.
   c. for two weeks' imprisonment for the guard and the secretary as her reward.

B. Read these lines from the play and answer the questions that follow.

1. **Secretary:** *The princess will see you. Remember, I get half of the reward.*
   Liza: *I have an excellent memory.*
   a. Why does the secretary want half of the reward?
   b. Why does Liza say that she has an excellent memory?
2. **Princess Margaret:** *Have you shown anyone?*
   Liza: *Not a soul, Your Majesty.*
   a. What is Princess Margaret asking Liza about?
   b. What does 'not a soul' mean there?

C. Answer these questions.

1. What did Liza see and find on a Sunday morning?
2. What did Liza decide to do?
3. Who stopped her at the royal palace?
4. What did Liza promise the guard and the secretary?
5. What was the second reward that Princess Margaret gave Liza?
6. How did Liza teach the gatekeeper and the secretary a lesson?

Life Skills and Values — **Honesty**

You must have spotted misplaced or lost items of stationery, water bottles, notebooks, etc. in the school premises. What should you do when you come across such items? Should you hand it over to the concerned authority, or should you just let it lie where you found it? Give reasons for your answer.

VOCABULARY

British and American English

- Although English is spoken worldwide, there are two distinct ways words are spelled.
- Some words are spelled differently in **British** and in **American** English. For example:

British English	*American English*
centre	*center*
cheque	*check*
colour	*color*
defence	*defense*
favour	*favor*
fibre	*fiber*
flavour	*flavor*
grey	*gray*
honour	*honor*
humour	*humor*
jewellery	*jewelry*
labour	*labor*
metre	*meter*
tyre	*tire*

A. Which spelling does each word in bold use? Write B for British or A for American spelling.

1. Mark wears **grey** T-shirts. ☐
2. Can I have a **litre** of milk, please? ☐
3. I wish to visit the Kennedy Space **Center.** ☐
4. Father went to the garage to change his car's **tyres.** ☐
5. What is your **favorite** TV programme? ☐
6. All the houses in the neighbourhood are the same **color.** ☐

Gender

- A word that refers to a male person or animal is of the **masculine gender**. For example:

  boy *man* *brother* *he* *bull* *peacock*

- A word that refers to a female person or animal is of the **feminine gender**. For example:

  girl *woman* *sister* *she* *cow* *peahen*

B. Change the gender of the words in bold and rewrite the passage.

The **princess** was very strong. **She** decided to protect **her** kingdom from the enemy. **She** led all **her** soldiers to the battleground and told **her father** not to worry about **her**. **Her mother**, who was a skilled archer, also encouraged **her** to go and fight for the kingdom.

GRAMMAR

Types of sentences

- A **sentence** is a group of words that makes complete sense, contains a main verb, and begins with a capital letter. There are four kinds of sentences.

Assertive or declarative sentence

- An **assertive sentence** states a fact or declares something.
- It ends with a full stop.

Jaya is a student. She lives in a big city.

Imperative sentence

- An **imperative sentence** gives a command or order.
- It usually ends with a full stop, but it may end with an exclamation mark.
- It is also used to make a request or express a wish.

Go to your room! (an order)

Please lend me your book. (a request)

Have a good time at the picnic. (a wish)

Exclamatory sentence

- An **exclamatory sentence** expresses a sudden and strong feeling, such as surprise, wonder, pity, fear, happiness, or gratitude.
- It usually ends with an exclamation mark.

What a shame!

How beautiful your garden looks!

Interrogative sentence

- An **interrogative sentence** asks a question.
- It always ends with a question mark.

What is your name?

Where do you live?

Read the sentences and identify their kind.

1. Nuremberg is in Germany. ....
2. How sweet the flower smells! ....
3. Please do visit the state museum. ....
4. Liza was a brave and smart girl. ....
5. Are you the girl who waves to me every Sunday? ....

LISTENING AND SPEAKING

Listening

A. Listen to two passages. Summarise each of them in one or two sentences.

1. ....

....

2. ....

....

Speaking

21st CENTURY SKILLS Critical Thinking

B. Look at the location of the church, Liza's house and the palace. Liza wants to reach the palace taking the shortest route. Study the route and give Liza directions to the palace.

You can use the following expressions:

- *Go straight.*
- *Look out for a bridge.*
- *Avoid the crowded market square.*
- *Take a left turn.*
- *Do not enter the forest.*

WRITING

Write a short review of the play *Liza and the Lost Letter*. Include the following information in the review.

- Who has written the play?
- Is the play set in modern times or old times?
- What is the play about?
- Who are the main characters in the play?
- Who is your favourite character and why?

PROJECT 3

The World of Stamps

When we post a letter, we need to stick a postage stamp on the envelope. Stamps are issued by the government of a country and are available at post offices.

Many people collect postage stamps as a hobby. The study and collection of postage stamps is called philately. Stamps tell us a lot about our culture and history. Each image printed on a stamp has a story to tell.

Ask your parents if they have any old stamps. Or, ask them to take you to a post office and let you buy five different stamps. Find out about the images on those stamps and make a mini stamp album. Each page should have the following:

- Actual stamp pasted on the top
- Name of the image printed on the stamp
- Significance of that image
- Value of the stamp

After you have made your album, take it to the class. Exchange your album with those of your classmates. Your class will now possess a huge collection of stamps.

Cross-Curricular Vocabulary

This section lists out all the new words used in the lessons, classified under cross-curricular categories.

Science

Plant world

bark: a tough protective outer layer of the trunk, branches, and twigs of a tree or woody shrub

blackberries: a small, soft fruit that grows on thorny bushes called brambles

blossom: all the flowers that appear on a tree before the fruit

ferns: flowerless plants with feathery leaves

foliage: the leaves of a plant considered collectively

leaflets: young leaves

nectar: a sweet liquid produced by flowers and collected by insects

Animal world

bulbuls: a tropical African and Asian songbird, typically having a tuft of feathers on the head, and a melodious voice

cud: partly digested food returned from the stomach of camels (as well as cattle, sheep, antelopes, deer and giraffes) to the mouth for further chewing

gazelle: a small antelope that has curved horns and a fawn-coloured coat with white underparts, found in Africa and Asia

minivets: an Asian songbird, the male of which is typically red and black, and the female yellow and grey

pedigreed: animals with recorded ancestry, showing they come from parents of the same breed or variety

praying mantis: a slender predatory insect with a triangular head, which waits motionless for prey with its large forelegs folded like hands in prayer

zoology: the scientific study of animals

Human body

allergic: caused by or related to an allergy

allergy: extreme sensitivity to a substance, especially a food, pollen, fur, or dust, which causes the body to react to it causing discomfort

Social Studies

Our earth

breezes: gentle winds

foothills: low hills at the base of a mountain or mountain range

mines: places where deep holes or tunnels are dug under the ground to extract coal, diamonds, gold, or other minerals

outskirts: the outer parts of a town or city

pebbles: small stones that are smooth and round

Art, culture, and heritage

Aesop's Fables: animal stories with a moral by Greek slave and storyteller Aesop who lived on the island of Samos during 6th century BC

canvas: a strong heavy cloth on which an artist does a painting

ceremony: a formal and traditional occasion, one celebrating an event

charcoals: paintings made using a black substance made by burning wood slowly in an oven with little air

duel: a formal fight with weapons between two people to settle a point of honour

enamel: a glossy substance applied on metallic or hard surfaces as a protective coating

engravings: images made by cutting designs on pieces of metal and then printing the designs on paper

goldsmith: a person who makes articles, such as jewellery

masterpiece: an excellent painting, novel, film or other work of art that has been made with great skill

mythological: relating to, based on, or appearing in myths or mythology

portraits: paintings, drawings, or photographs of someone, often of only their head and shoulders

procession: a group of people or vehicle moving together in a line, often as part of a ceremony

ritual: a solemn ceremony that consists of a series of actions performed as per a prescribed order

royal: belonging to a king, a queen, or a member of their family

silver-point: an old style of drawing by dragging a pointed silver wire across a surface

woodcuts: prints made from patterns cut in pieces of wood

Clothing and accesories

gumboots: long rubber boots

jumper: a warm knitted piece of clothing which covers the upper part of your body and your arms

robes: long loose outer garments reaching to the ankles

Different Parts of Speech

Nouns

adoption: the action of legally taking up another's child or an animal and bringing it up as one's own

alley: American word for a narrow passageway between or behind buildings

appointments secretary: a person who works under another person and arranges his/her meetings

barrel: a wooden container with rounded sides and flat ends

carrier: a basket-like case for transporting small pets

casket: a small box or chest for keeping jewels, letters, or valued objects

cat tree: an artificial structure made of wood and covered with carpet for cats to play, exercise and relax on

commissioner: the head of a city administration

copper: a soft reddish-brown metal used for making electric wires, coins, etc.

directive: an official instruction given by somebody in authority

discussions: conversations about a specific topic

enclosure: an area that is closed off with a fence

granary: a building used for storing grain

grief: deep sorrow, especially caused by someone's death

haunt: a place frequently visited by a person

homage: special honour or respect shown publicly

homecoming: an occasion of returning home

household: a house and its occupants regarded as a unit

imposter: a person who is pretending to be someone else to trick people

intention: an aim or plan made in advance

lifeline: a thing on which someone or something depends on or which provides a means of escape from a difficult situation

litter: a material used to line a shallow container which is used by cats as an indoor toilet

miracle: a wonderful and surprising event, especially one believed to be caused by God

outhouse: a building such as a shed that is built on or in the grounds of a house

popularity: the state of being liked by many people

responsibility: a moral duty that one is required to do, such as take care of someone or something

safari: a trip to see wild animals

settee: a long seat with a back and arms

sidewalk: American word for pavement

sprinkling: a small thinly distributed amount

swarm: a large number

tarpaulin: a strong waterproof cloth, originally of canvas

trash: American word for garbage or waste material

tribute: something said or done to show admiration and respect for someone

urchin: a young child who is poorly or raggedly dressed

warmth: the quality, state, or sensation of being warm; moderate heat

will: a legal document containing instructions as to what should be done with one's money and property after one's death

Adjectives

bulging: swelling

crowded: full of people, leaving little or no room for movement; packed

curious: eager to know or learn something

dangerous: something which is likely to cause harm or injury

eager: strongly wanting to do or have something; keen

festive: relating to a festival; cheerful and celebratory

financial: relating to money

formation: the pattern or shape of something

futile: having no purpose because there is no chance of success; pointless

grim: unpleasant and depressing

imprinted: stamped on the surface with a mark or outline

just: fair or right

lush: (gardens) with a lot of green grass or plants

masterful: showing great skill

memorable: worth remembering or easily remembered, especially because of being special or unusual

ornate: richly decorated with patterns and designs

predefined: defined or established in advance

scarlet: of a brilliant red colour

scorching: very hot

severe: very great; intense

sheltered: (a place) protected from bad weather

silly: foolish; unimportant

slender: thin or narrow

splendid: wonderful

stoutest: strongest and thickest

stunted: prevented the normal growth or development

tang: a strong taste or flavour

timid: showing a lack of courage and confidence

vain: arrogant; extremely proud

yielding: not hard or rigid

Verbs

abused: mistreated

accommodate: to do a favour; adapt or adjust

begged: asked or requested sincerely

behold: to see; look at (old English)

beset: affected in an unpleasant or harmful way

brace: (take) a firm position

ceased: stopped

clung: held on tightly

coax: to persuade someone gradually or gently to do something

compensate: to pay someone for work performed

conquer: to defeat; to succeed in dealing with or doing something

desert: to go away; to leave

enquired: asked for information

enrol: to officially register to join or become a member of an institution or a student on a course

ensure: to make certain that something happens

escorted: went with another to protect or guide them

fared: performed (at a task)

feasting: eating and/or drinking in large quantities

fret: to worry about something

glanced: gave a brief or hurried look

grinning: smiling broadly

groom: to clean the fur or skin by licking

huddled: crowded together in a small space

indulge: to let someone have or do what they want

jangle: to make or cause to make a ringing metallic sound

jerked: made a quick, sharp, or sudden movement

petted: stroked or patted lovingly

piled: placed one on top of the other

pouting: pushing one's lips forward as an expression of annoyance

pursue: to follow or chase (someone or something)

rear: to care for an animal's young ones until they are fully grown

reconsidered: thought about something again

resumed: started doing something again after a break

retrieved: brought out something from somewhere

rustling: making a soft, muffled sound like that caused by the movement of dry leaves

scolded: told someone off angrily after finding fault with them

scowls: frowns in an angry or bad-tempered way

shivers: shakes slightly and uncontrollably because of being cold, frightened, or excited

smashed: violently or badly broken or shattered

snuggle: to settle into a warm, comfortable position

soothe: to gently calm a person or their feelings

stared: looked fixedly at someone or something with one's eyes wide open

summon: to order someone to come

tucked: put in a secure manner

urge: to persistently persuade someone to do something

whispered: spoke very softly using one's breath rather than one's throat

wolfed: ate quickly and greedily

Verbs related to movement

belted: moved somewhere very quickly

dismounted: got off a vehicle, a horse, or anything that one is riding

dodge: to move quickly to one side to avoid something; to avoid doing something

flitted: moved swiftly and lightly from one place to another

flopped: sat down heavily and suddenly

fluttering: moving with a light irregular or trembling motion

frolicked: played or moved about in a cheerful and lively way
plodded: walked slowly with heavy steps
streaming: moving in a continuous flow
striding: walking with long, decisive steps in a specified direction
strut: to walk in a proud way with your head held high and your chest out

Adverbs

briskly: quickly
immediately: at once; without delay
promptly: immediately; without any delay
squarely: directly
vaguely: slightly

Feeling words

anticipation: looking forward to
anxious: feeling worried or nervous
confident: feeling sure about one's abilities
crosser: angrier; more annoyed
embarrassed: felt shy or ashamed
grumpy: bad-tempered and irritable
impatient: annoyed or irritated because you do not want to wait for someone or something
merry: happy
uncomfortable: worried or nervous

Phrases and idioms

empty apology: saying sorry without meaning it
in trim: in good condition